Sandra Kendo
Editor

Non-Financial Reporting and ESG Performance

Standards, Challenges and Impacts for the SME of Tomorrow

palgrave
macmillan

Editor
Sandra Kendo
ICL, Junia, Université Catholique de Lille, LITL
Lille, France

ISSN 2662-5105 ISSN 2662-5113 (electronic)
Palgrave Studies in Impact Finance
ISBN 978-3-032-19091-8 ISBN 978-3-032-19092-5 (eBook)
https://doi.org/10.1007/978-3-032-19092-5

This Palgrave Macmillan imprint is published by the registered company Springer Nature Switzerland AG.
The registered company address is: Gewerbestrasse 11, 6330 Cham, Switzerland.

Palgrave Studies in Impact Finance

Series Editor
Mario La Torre, Department of Management,
Sapienza University of Rome, Rome, Italy

The *Palgrave Studies in Impact Finance* series provides a valuable scientific "hub" for researchers, professionals and policy makers involved in Impact finance and related topics. It includes studies in the social, political, environmental and ethical impact of finance, exploring all aspects of impact finance and socially responsible investment, including policy issues, financial instruments, markets and clients, standards, regulations and financial management, with a particular focus on impact investments and microfinance.

Titles feature the most recent empirical analysis with a theoretical approach, including up to date and innovative studies that cover issues which impact finance and society globally.

I dedicate this book first and foremost to my daddy, "Joseph Tchakounte," whose unwavering support and encouragement guided me throughout my journey in research and teaching. Although he left us too soon, I know he would have been proud to witness this collaborative work with my colleagues, whose professionalism, patience, and kindness were invaluable.
I also specially and delightfully dedicate this book to my mommy, Mrs "Jeannette Tchakounte"; my sisters, Rosine, Solange, Christelle, Josephine, and Nathalie, as well as my nieces, nephews, brother, and brothers-in-law, Annaelle, Grâce-Jade, Jared, Ariel, Jérémie, Darios, Marcel, Joël, and Ivan.
A special Smile filled with Hope, Joy, Gratitude, and LOVE to all my friends and colleagues whom I truly cherish … Our success is also yours….
I would like to specifically mention the most recent addition to the team, Thanh-Tuan Nguyen, an Associate Professor in the field of sustainability, who obtained his Ph.D. in December 2025, and whose valuable contributions helped consolidate the ideas and analyses presented in this book. The last but not the least….
A special dedication goes to our Dean of the faculty (FGES-EDN-ISEA), Sophie Cavillon, whose patience, kindness, wisdom, compassion, and encouragement inspire the entire team.

Sandra Kendo

Foreword

Small and medium-sized enterprises (SMEs) constitute the backbone of economic activity in nearly every country. They account for close to 90% of businesses worldwide and generate more than half of total employment (World Bank, https://www.worldbank.org/en/topic/smefinance). Owing to their economic weight, their capacity to develop and diffuse innovation, and their local and collective impact, SMEs play a crucial role in shaping a more sustainable future.

Businesses face increasing expectations to explain how their activities affect the environment and society at large. The European Union—and, to varying degrees, governments around the world—now requires large companies to publish detailed information on their environmental, social, and governance (ESG) performance through non-financial reporting (NFR) obligations. SMEs, in contrast, generally benefit from reduced or voluntary reporting requirements. However, many choose to engage in sustainability reporting to strengthen transparency, reputation, and stakeholder trust.

In practice, sustainability reporting demands resources that smaller firms often lack. Preparing non-financial reports requires dedicated staff with the necessary expertise, reliable information systems to define and monitor indicators, and organizational capacity to integrate sustainability into daily operations. For many SMEs, these requirements are difficult to meet—especially in the absence of a dedicated unit responsible for ESG strategy and actions.

While multinational corporations have long been at the forefront of ESG disclosure, SMEs are increasingly recognized as indispensable actors in this transition. Yet, their journey toward sustainability is marked by specific challenges: limited internal resources, technical and methodological complexity, and a perceived imbalance between reporting requirements and organizational capability. At the same time, SMEs possess immense potential—as innovators, as partners within supply chains, and as key players in local sustainability ecosystems.

This book, "*Non-Financial Reporting and ESG Performance: Standards, Challenges and Impact for the SME of Tomorrow,*" addresses a crucial issue: how ESG principles and non-financial reporting initiatives can be integrated to facilitate the adoption of sustainability practices among SMEs. The main factors that motivate smaller firms to engage in ESG and NFR initiatives, as we will see, can be grouped into four primary drivers: legitimacy, competitive advantage, stakeholder pressure, and stakeholder engagement. In other words, SMEs act to maintain or enhance their legitimacy, strengthen brand value and reputation, attract and retain clients—particularly larger enterprises that evaluate suppliers based on their sustainability credentials—and mobilize internal and external stakeholders such as employees, investors, local communities, and customers.

The likelihood of SMEs engaging in sustainability practices also depends on the broader environment in which they operate. Enabling conditions—such as clear and proportionate guidelines adapted to SMEs' needs, as well as practical tools and frameworks—can significantly ease the implementation of non-financial reporting.

The goal of this book is to provide accessible pathways for SMEs to structure their ESG reporting and performance management. It begins by examining how the concept of Corporate Social Responsibility (CSR) has evolved over time and how regulatory developments have shaped contemporary ESG practices. It then explores the relationship between ESG performance and both financial and non-financial outcomes. Building on these foundations, the book introduces methodological tools to operationalize ESG measurement, including a structured approach for calculating a composite ESG indicator. This approach responds to the ongoing challenge of achieving comparability and standardization in ESG assessment while ensuring scalability and proportionality for smaller organizations.

Subsequent chapters investigate how environmental, social, and governance dimensions can be integrated into SMEs' business models. Through case studies, the book highlights both the operational challenges and the transformative potential of aligning business strategies with sustainability objectives. The final chapters focus on regulatory developments—particularly within the European Union—where evolving standards are reshaping accounting and reporting practices for SMEs. These sections conclude with detailed case studies that demonstrate practical approaches to embedding ESG principles into corporate strategy. The examples underscore recurring challenges such as resource constraints, data complexity, and continuous adaptation to new standards, while also showing how incremental and pragmatic sustainability initiatives can generate competitive and relational advantages.

What makes this book particularly valuable is its holistic perspective. It does not treat ESG reporting merely as a compliance exercise, but as a transformative process capable of driving strategic renewal and value creation. By bridging theory and practice, it offers a comprehensive framework for understanding how SMEs can meaningfully engage with sustainability.

Looking ahead, the SME of tomorrow will be defined not only by financial performance but also by its capacity to create sustainable economic, social, and environmental value. The ability to measure and communicate that value transparently will become a decisive factor in accessing markets, securing financing, and ensuring long-term resilience. Non-financial reporting is therefore not simply a regulatory trend—it is a cornerstone for building more responsible businesses and stronger, more inclusive societies.

This book invites readers—scholars, practitioners, and policymakers alike—to embrace this vision. By connecting emerging standards with the lived realities of SMEs, it offers both analytical insight and practical guidance, contributing to a more sustainable and inclusive future.

France, Lille, 2025 — Véronique Flambard

Preface

This proposed collective work results from three years of research conducted by a multidisciplinary team on the CICAMI project, from October 2022 to March 2026, at the Catholic University of Lille. Among them are the *Mouvement des Entreprises de France Hauts-de-France*, a key player in the regional economic fabric, and *TEAM2*, an innovation ecosystem specializing in the circular economy. The *Fondation de la Catho de Lille* also provides its academic and scientific expertise. At the same time, *Autonomie et Solidarité (A&S)* plays a crucial role in accompanying and supporting companies undergoing this transition. In addition to these partnerships, we have a team of 12 researchers who are mobilised, led by Sandra Kendo, whom I would like to thank for her important work.

The insights presented in this book are vital for helping small and medium-sized enterprises (SMEs) transition to a more sustainable and resilient economy. The proposed structured framework allows companies to enhance their overall performance, secure their operations, attract responsible financing, and meet the growing regulatory requirements..

Through this concerted reflection, it becomes apparent that there is a need to foster close collaboration among companies, investors, and researchers to enhance sustainability practices. The dedication of the researchers involved, along with my role as dean in this project, has enabled us to provide the necessary resources for conducting this operational research. Additionally, we are working to establish a School/Business Hub that will enhance the dialogue between the academic and economic sectors. The various companies in the region that participated in this study expressed a strong interest in a better understanding of the issues related to the regulatory framework, the application of ESG issues in the production trajectory and the deployment of new business models.

What if we could develop an ESG index explicitly tailored for SMEs to enhance their understanding of ESG performance and challenges?

Today, most ESG guidelines and datasets are primarily developed for large companies. Meanwhile, small and medium-sized enterprises (SMEs) often struggle to implement sustainable practices due to limited financial and human resources. This challenge led us, "a group of researchers, professors, and sustainability practitioners," to initiate a research project aimed at supporting SMEs in developing their own CSR and ESG strategies by creating an ESG index for SMEs in the Hauts-de-France region.

We begin by exploring the foundations of CSR and ESG, their historical development, and their connections with corporate theories and financial performance, framed through three literature-based chapters. In Chapter 4, we introduce our ESG index for SMEs, which is built on empirical fieldwork and a questionnaire specifically developed for small and medium-sized enterprises. The final chapters present real case studies, illustrating how ESG principles are integrated into SME business models and how ESG accounting is applied in practice.

This book is a call to *rethink sustainability at the SME level.* Our goal is to make a meaningful contribution to literature in sustainable and corporate finance by proposing new analytical tools and offering grounded, real-world insights.

In a world facing urgent environmental and social challenges, there is a critical need for *more conscious investors, decision-makers, and policymakers.* Only through collective awareness and action can we truly achieve the Sustainable Development Goals and shape a better future for generations to come.

France, Lille, 2025 Sophie Cavillon

Acknowledgments

We would first like to express our sincere gratitude to the Région Hauts-de-France, and in particular to *Xavier Bertrand*, *Christelle Demaretz*, and *Eric Staniek*, for their financial support of the CICAMI project and for enabling us to carry out this impactful work.

We also extend our thanks to the Institut Catholique de Lille and La Fondation de la Catho de Lille, especially to *Patrick Scauflaire*, *Nicolas Valliant*, *Bénédicte Paree*, and *Didier Peillon*, for their financial support, continued trust, and institutional recognition and efforts.

Our appreciation also goes to the Faculté de Gestion, Économie & Sciences (FGES) for their encouragement, advice, and for sharing their thoughts throughout the project. We are grateful to *Sophie Cavillon*, *Véronique Flambard-Vigeant*, *Claire Dufossé*, *Johanne Pollaert*, *Sadia Benamrouz Vanneste*, *Patricia Morocho*, *Anne-Sophie Rogez-Theeten*, as well as all our faculty colleagues and the administrative team. We thank *Laurent Lamoine* for his valuable early contributions, which helped align the core objectives and research questions of the project.

A special thanks is due to the entire CICAMI team for taking on the challenge and contributing as authors to this book, which reflects the project's journey and achievements.

We warmly acknowledge our partners at Autonomie et Solidarité (A & S): *Arnaud Bernard*, *Marie-Christine Lenain*, *Hélène Ostrowski*, and *Maïté Lecocq*, without whom this collaboration would not have been possible.

Finally, we express our appreciation to *Tula Weis*, Executive Editor at Palgrave Macmillan, for her valuable feedback, guidance, and support throughout the publication process.

Stéphanie Lodieu

Competing Interest This study was funded by the Institut *Catholique de Lille* and made possible by financial support from the *Région Hauts-de-France.*

Sandra Kendo, the coordinator of the research project, has received the research grant.

The author has no conflicts of interest to declare that are relevant to the content of the book.

Ethics Approval This study was performed in line with the principles of the Declaration of Helsinki. Approval was granted by the Ethics Committee of Université Catholique de Lille.

December 14, 2025

Notes on Contributors

Jean Claude Brou, Associate Professor, ESG Finance—Galileo Global Education, France. Expert in macroeconomics, public finance, and applied econometrics. His analyses also incorporate issues of sustainable development and digitalization, notably in SMEs/TPEs as well as in the agricultural sector. His work has been published in *Applied Economics*, *Economic Systems*, and *Journal of Economic Integration*.

Sophie Cavillon, Professor of Biology specializing in plant physiology and molecular biology, and currently Dean of the Faculté Libre des Sciences et Technologies (ICL). Since joining the faculty in 2004, she has combined teaching with a strong commitment to academic leadership. As program director of the Life Sciences degree, she contributed to the creation of a successful Biotechnology track. In 2018, she became Vice-Dean for Pedagogy and Academic Affairs, coordinating undergraduate programs and fostering innovation in teaching. Appointed Deputy Dean in 2023 and elected Dean in 2024, she continue to promote the development of our faculty at both national and international levels, while strengthening partnerships and ensuring the well-being of students and staff.

Nejwa Elalami, Master 1 Intern on the research applied project CICAMI at *Université Catholique de Lille*.

Véronique Flambard, Professor of Economics, at the Faculty of Management Economics and Sciences (FGES) in Université Catholique de Lille. She is also the director of LITL (Laboratory of Interdisciplinary Transition of Lille), a research center of Université Catholique de Lille. She conducts research in environmental economics, with a particular focus on energy efficiency, behavioral economics, and the impact of public policies in the areas of housing and energy sobriety.

Safia Gherab, Master 1 Intern on the research applied project CICAMI at *Université Catholique de Lille.*

Fatma Guneri, Associate professor in Management Sciences at LIDD Ecole du Design and membre of Laboratoire Interdisciplinaire des Transitions de Lille at Université Catholique de Lille. Her research area includes expertise in Workspace and new ways of organizing Work in Anthropocene era.

Oussama Kacemi, Oussama Kacemi is an economist specializing in applied economic analysis, and a research engineer at *Université Catholique de Lille.* His research adopts a quantitative approach, drawing on econometrics, statistics, and modeling to shed light on contemporary issues related to environmental and development economics.

Marie-Renée Loucou, Master 1 Intern on the research applied project CICAMI at *Université Catholique de Lille.*

Marion Mauchaussee, Associate professor at *Université Catholique de Lille* as labor economist. She works primarily on public sector employment practices and labor movements in the private labor market. However, she also incorporates an environmental dimension into her research, analyzing the dynamics of mobility towards green industries.

Hélène Ostrowski, Business Manager at Autonomy and Solidarity (A&S).

Sandra Ramos, Associate Professor in Management Sciences at Université Catholique de Lille. She obtained her PhD in 2019, focusing on the role of human capital in the failure of social enterprises. Her research interests include entrepreneurship and social enterprises, organizational failure, and, more recently, the transformation of business models.

Jean Daniel Wecxsteen, Director of ISEA (Institut Supérieur d'Expertise et d'Audit), *Université Catholique de Lille*. Before joining ISEA, Jean Daniel was working in the banking sector as a director. He is also working in economics. In addition, as director, through my responsibilities as academic advisor of the Master's in Law and Wealth Management (DGP), I have the opportunity to develop, mobilize, and strengthen a network of experts, accountants, and financial directors in connection with the challenges of extra-financial reporting and green & sustainable accounting.

Baran Siyahhan, Associate Professor of Finance at *Université Catholique de Lille* and a member of the LITL research center. He holds a PhD in Finance from Vienna University Economics and Business (2010). His research interests include sustainable finance, corporate investment and financing decisions and industrial organization.

Ivan Terraglia, Ivan Terraglia is a PhD student at the University of Teramo, undertaking studies in Economic and Social Sciences. His research focuses on quantifying sustainability through the application of statistical indicators. He was a visiting PhD student at Lille Catholic University. His work has been published in journals such as *Socio-Economic Planning Sciences*, *Social Indicators Research*, *Big Data Research*, and *Quality & Quantity*.

Qing Xu, Associate Professor at Université Catholique de Lille. Qing XU is a member of the LITL research center and an associate member of the GREDEG research team. She obtained her PhD in Economics from Université Côte d'Azur in 2014. Her research focuses primarily on mobile payment systems in Asia and Africa, with particular interest in the transferability of these models to other countries. She also works on topics related to fintech development, digital currencies, sustainable finance and ESG issues.

Wissal Zribi, postdoctoral researcher in sustainable finance at *Université Catholique de Lille*. She has also been a visiting researcher at IPAG Business School and Paris School of Business. Her research focuses on the intersection of sustainability, the financial sphere, and uncertainty. Her work has been published in journals such as the *International Review of Financial Analysis*, *Finance Research Letters*, and the *Journal of Economic Asymmetries*.

About the Editor

Sandra Kendo is an Associate Professor of Monetary Economics and Banking at the Catholic University of Lille and holds the Chair in Business Ethics focused on Compliance, ESG, and Non-Financial Reporting. Her updated research addresses ESG and non-financial risks, corporate investment, and financial stability, with a focus on banks and SMEs. Through the Chair, she advances research in ESG analysis and develops non-financial reporting frameworks tailored to firms' economic constraints.

Since January 2023, she has led a funded applied research-action project (2023–2026)[1] to develop a composite financial and non-financial index that measures SMEs' engagement in ESG practices, using original survey data. The project is supported by the Catholic University of Lille with funding from the Department of the Hauts-de-France.

Her research builds on previous work in banking structure, competition, and financing capacity, and has been published in *Empirical Economics*, *The Quarterly Review of Economics and Finance*, and *Applied Economics*. She contributes methodologically through advanced econometric techniques, especially panel and quantile regression. Her current work explores ESG and political risks, alternative risk indices, and data-driven approaches such as machine learning to evaluate their effects on corporate performance and financial stability.
https://orcid.org/0000-0002-8549-5414

[1] https://litl-lab.fr/cicami/

Contents

Abbreviations

ACPR	Autorité de Contrôle Prudentiel et de Résolution
AFG	Association française de la gestion financière
AGEC	Anti-Gaspillage pour une Economie Circulaire
AMF	Autorité des Marchés Financiers
ANC	Autorité des Normes Comptables
AUM	Assets Under Management
BMs	Business Models
CapEx	Capital Expenditure
CARE	Comprehensive Accounting in Respect of Ecology
CEO	Chief Executive Officer
CERES	Coalition for Environmentally Responsible Economies
CERCES	Cercle des Comptables Environnementaux et Sociaux
CFP	Corporate Financial Performance
CO_2	Carbon dioxide
CSDD	Corporate Sustainability Due Diligence Directive
CSP	Corporate Social Performance
CSR	Corporate Social Responsibility
CSRD	Corporate Sustainability Reporting Directive
CSV	Creating Shared Value
DJSI	Dow Jones Sustainability Index
DNSH	Do No Significant Harm
EAP	Environmental Action Program

EFRAG	European Financial Reporting Advisory Group
EPA	Environmental Protection Agency
ESG CI	ESG Composite Index
ESG	environmental, social, governance
ESRS	European Sustainability Reporting Standards
ESS	Social and Solidarity Economy
EU	European Union
Eurosif	European Sustainable Investment Forum
GDP	Gross Domestic Product
GFC	Global Financial Crisis
GLP	Green Loan Principles
GRI	Global Reporting Initiative
IAS	International Accounting Standards
IASB	International Accounting Standards Board
IFRS	International Financial Reporting Standards
ISSB	International Sustainability Standards Board
M&As	Mergers and Acquisitions
MNCs	Multinational Companies
MPI	Mazziotta-Pareto Index
MSMEs	Micro, Small, and Medium-sized Enterprises
NFRD	Non-Financial Reporting Directive
NGFS	Network for Greening the Financial System
NGOs	Non-Governmental Organizations
NRE	Nouvelles Régulations Économiques
OECD	Organisation for Economic Co-operation and Development
OpEx	Operating Expenditure
QWL	Quality of Work Life
RBV	Resource-Based View
RI	Responsible Investment
RIL	Responsible Investment Label
ROA	Return On Asset
SASB	Sustainability Accounting Standards Board
SBM	Sustainable Business Model
SCSR	Strategic CSR
SDGs	Sustainable Development Goals
SeMA	Sense-Making Accounting
SFDR	Sustainable Finance Disclosure Regulation
SLBs	sustainability-linked bonds
SME	Small, and Medium-sized Enterprises
SNDD	Stratégie Nationale de Déveleppement Durable
SRI	socially responsible investment
SWOT	Strengths, Weaknesses, Opportunities, Threats
TCFD	Task Force on Climate-related Financial Disclosures

TOWS	Threats, Opportunities, Weaknesses, Strengths
UNEP	United Nations Environment Program
UNFCCC	United Nations Framework Convention on Climate Change
US	United States
YMCA	Young Men's Christian Association

List of Figures

List of Tables

Introduction

The integration of sustainability into risk-profitability analysis can enhance the environmental, social, and governance (ESG) potential performance of companies. Additionally, various improvements in non-financial reporting, primarily based on ESG considerations, have emerged. These issues are particularly relevant for small and medium-sized enterprises (SMEs) and micro-enterprises. A critical observation is the extensive range of alternative tools and expert resources available to large companies, which assist managers and boards in addressing complex questions related to risk, profitability, and sustainability, as well as in communicating ESG engagement through non-financial reporting. In contrast, approaches for SMEs and micro-enterprises require further consolidation to provide actionable insights for managers, investors, and policymakers within these sectors.

During our applied research study, which involved collecting primary data in the Northern part of France, we observed that the growth and development of the Hauts-de-France region's economy were initially and primarily based on the development of industrial activities in the textile, steel, and mining industries. The development of these industrial activities has had a considerable impact on the economic, social, and environmental landscapes of the region. Although we have observed positive externalities on the economic and social fabric, negative externalities on the environment have also been noted. Taking into account positive externalities is an important dimension to consider in a financing process that integrates both societal and environmental considerations. A gradual and significant deterioration of the green belt and our ecosystem has prompted a considerable shift in reflection on new economic development models that incorporate these aspects. The current new economic models promote a green economy, a circular economy, a functional economy, and/or a social and solidarity economy.

Sustainable development is based on an intercorrelated balance of these different models. In the context of our study, we primarily focus on the importance of articulating solidarity with the circular economy, particularly the new business development model that combines financial profitability with social, societal, and/or environmental impact. This proposed approach aims to analyze and evaluate the balance model between *Risk, Profitability, and Sustainability*, for small and medium enterprises (SMEs). The objective is to develop a strategy that integrates financial and non-financial indicators to measure companies' overall performance more effectively, thereby supporting their transition to a more sustainable economic model.

In a forward-looking approach to the sustainable and long-term development of companies in industrial regions with similar characteristics to those of Hauts-de-France, it is necessary to rethink the balance between risk and profitability, integrating non-financial issues of a solidarity nature, particularly the environmental, social/societal, and governance dimensions. In this regard, the increasingly important role of consistency in benchmark analyses for investors and policymakers is crucial for ensuring the optimization of information related to company performance and achieving sustainable development goals. The Autorité des Marchés Financiers (AMF) in France places particular emphasis on the need to combine financial and non-financial information to gain a more comprehensive view of the determinants of company performance. Considering environmental, social, and governance (ESG) criteria would contribute to observing different levels of profitability, with risk levels being weighted or mitigated by the valuation of ESG criteria. Generally, a high level of risk is associated with a high level of profitability, coupled with an investment that is not necessarily of a joint and several nature, and vice versa.

On the eve of various crises, such as the 2008 financial crisis and the COVID-19 crisis of 2020, there has been a focus on the availability of essential goods and services. Following the COVID-19 crisis and the increased consideration of the Paris Agreement in 2015, investors and companies alike have emphasized improving the stability and sustainability of their businesses, along with the growing need for environmental, social, and governance (ESG) reporting (Gholami et al., 2022). Over the past two decades, the literature has undergone an enrichment, focusing more on the relationship between companies' ESG performance and their financial performance. Some empirical studies (e.g., Krüger 2015; Di Giuli & Kostovetsky, 2014) highlight a non-significant or insignificant relationship between ESG performance and financial performance. Other empirical work reveals a positive and meaningful relationship between ESG performance and corporate performance. For example, socially responsible firms have demonstrated higher resilience during systemic shocks (Lins, Servaes, and Tamayo, 2017; Albuquerque, Koskinen, and Zhang, 2019) and firm-specific shocks, such as negative actions related to firm operations (Ho, Nguyen, and Vu, 2020; Aouadi & Marsat, 2018). Additionally, investments in CSR and improved ESG performance can help mitigate conflicts of interest among companies' stakeholders (Harjoto & Jo, 2011). As a result, firms can establish a closer relationship with consumers who are willing to accept higher prices (Wei et al., 2018; Castro-Gonzalez et al., 2021).

The company's share capital reinforces the degree of confidence that shareholders can have. The degree of confidence revealed in broad daylight during periods of crisis is through the undeniable support provided by these shareholder investors. There are two significant challenges in the literature and practice related to ESG performance. The first challenge is related to assessing companies' ESG performance. Several indicators provided by third parties include the Dow Jones Sustainability Index (DJSI), Bloomberg ESG Data Service, and MSCI ESG Research. These indices are very often used by wealth managers and academic researchers (Bardos et al., 2021; Giese et al., 2019) to analyze the performance of listed companies. The abundance of different patterns leads to a divergence in company ratings (Christensen et al., 2022). The second challenge is on the type of companies considered. Most studies on non-financial ratings and ESG standards present results from listed companies, with very few studies focusing on VSEs/SMEs (Gholami et al., 2022). It is essential to enhance the impact measurements by incorporating more VSEs/SMEs into the analysis, as they are not only a significant niche for employment in various regional localities but also a key driver in transforming the economic and entrepreneurial ecosystem.

This book seeks to enhance our reflection by presenting a variety of topics for consideration. The first one is to outline the regulatory framework, including various European measures and directives related to ESG issues, as well as the definition of a non-financial reporting framework (Chap. 1). Then, to present the challenges and issues for investors in considering non-financial reporting standards when developing investments, and the expected sustainable performance of the portfolio (Chap. 2). Thirdly, the understanding of the ESG legal framework enables the introduction of a combined and enriching perspective, incorporating foresight and economic thinking in relation to ESG performance, through the application of three theoretical frameworks: neo-institutional theory, stakeholder theory, and signal theory (Chap. 3). Based on these initial reflections, we propose a starting point for developing an appropriate methodological approach to implement for an ESG performance analysis of small and medium-sized companies (SMEs), based on primary survey data collected (Chap. 4). We complete this theoretical analysis with two additional parts presenting the transformations of business models with the appearance of new business models systematically integrating ESG criteria (Chap. 5) and at last, we address the concept of green accounting, sustainable accounting, how SMEs integrate these new accounting approaches, and how this transforms the landscape of the accounting evolution of their activity (Chap. 6).

References

Albuquerque, R., Koskinen, Y., & Zhang, C. (2019). Corporate social responsibility and firm risk: Theory and empirical evidence. *Management Science, 65*(10), 4451–4469.

Aouadi, A., & Marsat, S. (2018). Do ESG controversies matter for firm value? Evidence from international data. *Journal of Business Ethics, 151*(4), 1027–1047.

Bardos, K. S., Ertugrul, M., & Gao, L. S. (2020). Corporate social responsibility, product market perception, and firm value. *Journal of Corporate Finance, 62*, 101588.

Castro-González, S., Bande, B., & Fernández-Ferrín, P. (2021). Influence of companies' credibility and trust in corporate social responsibility aspects of consumer food products: The moderating intervention of consumer integrity. *Sustainable Production and Consumption, 28*, 129–141.

Christensen, D. M., Serafeim, G., & Sikochi, A. (2022). Why is corporate virtue in the eye of the beholder? The case of ESG ratings. *The Accounting Review, 97*(1), 147–175.

D'Amato, V., D'Ecclesia, R., & Levantesi, S. (2021). Fundamental ratios as predictors of ESG scores: A machine learning approach. *Decisions in Economics and Finance, 44*(2), 1087–1110.

Gangi, F., Meles, A., Monferrà, S., & Mustilli, M. (2020). Does corporate social responsibility help the survivorship of SMEs and large firms? *Global Finance Journal, 43*, 100402.

Gholami, A., Murray, P. A., & Sands, J. (2022). Environmental, social, governance & financial performance disclosure for large firms: Is this different for SME firms? *Sustainability, 14*(10), 6019.

Giese, G., Lee, L. E., Melas, D., Nagy, Z., & Nishikawa, L. (2019). Foundations of ESG investing: How ESG affects equity valuation, risk, and performance. *The Journal of Portfolio Management, 45*(5), 69–83.

Harjoto, M. A., & Jo, H. (2011). Corporate governance and CSR nexus. *Journal of Business Ethics, 100*(1), 45–67.

Ho, C. C., Nguyen, H., & Vu, V. H. (2020). Do environmental and social risks affect corporate financial policies? SSRN. https://doi.org/10.2139/ssrn.3601616

CHAPTER 1

Corporate Social Responsibility and ESG Directives

Wissal Zribi, Marion Mauchaussee, and Jean Claude Brou

Abstract This chapter establishes the conceptual and historical foundations of ESG by tracing the evolution of Corporate Social Responsibility (CSR) as an antecedent to modern sustainability reporting. Structured in two main sections, it first explores the origin of CSR, from the early philanthropic initiatives before 1950 to the post-COVID-19 era of integrated responsibility. Anchored in seminal academic contributions including Bowen (1953), Frederick (1960), Carroll (1977; 1991; 2008), and Smith (2009), the chapter examines how definitions of CSR have expanded over time to encompass economic, managerial, and socio-cultural dimensions. The theoretical underpinnings of CSR are presented through the lens of stakeholder theory and the shifting expectations of corporate accountability in society.

W. Zribi
ICL, Junia, Université Catholique de Lille, LITL, Lille France

M. Mauchaussee (✉)
ICL, Junia, Université Catholique de Lille, LITL
e-mail: marion.mauchausse@univ-catholille.fr

J.-C. Brou
ESG Finance, Courbevoie, France

S. Kendo (ed.), *Non-Financial Reporting and ESG Performance*, Palgrave Studies in Impact Finance,
https://doi.org/10.1007/978-3-032-19092-5_1

The second section addresses the regulatory and institutional trajectory that has shaped ESG practices today. It outlines the progressive stages in the formalization of CSR directives, starting with the emergence of voluntary guidelines in the 1970s–1990s, followed by the expansion of formal frameworks and global initiatives in the 2000s. The 2010s marked a shift toward mandatory disclosure mechanisms and regionally enforced accountability, culminating in the current era of harmonization and ESG integration. This final phase reflects a broader consensus around global sustainability imperatives, supported by policy innovations and increased stakeholder pressure.

Keywords ESG • CSR • Compliance • Non-Financial Reporting

1.1 Introduction

Following the Industrial Revolution that marked the nineteenth century, many companies had to confront the damage their activities caused to society. A new concept emerged in business jargon and language, aimed at minimizing the negative impact by enhancing the positive side of actions and companies on society: Corporate Social Responsibility (CSR). Since then, this concept has been regularly discussed and has become a topic of debate and study among researchers. The debate on the topic of corporate social responsibility is rich thanks to its multidisciplinary nature (history, philosophy, economics, sociology, management science), and due to the diverse backgrounds of the authors of the publications, the various institutions, and the corporate approaches. The theme of CSR has been considered a new arena for action for businesses, with new actors developing new managerial rhetoric and practices.

The 2008 financial crisis, with its economic and social consequences, led many experts, politicians, and business leaders to call for collective mobilization in favor of greater corporate social responsibility, in its various aspects (the three ESG dimensions: environmental, social, and governance). They view it as an opportunity to revise the nineteenth-century business model and introduce new dynamics of inclusive and sustainable growth. The European Commission calls on states to adopt a resolutely "strategic" approach to CSR/ESG dimensions, to reconcile the demands of social responsibility and competitiveness. This awareness of social, environmental, and governance concerns has increased at the corporate level, contributing to a rise in the volume of voluntary corporate social responsibility initiatives and codes of business conduct. These initiatives were designed to help organizations create strategies, indicators, or principles that reflect a CSR and sustainable development philosophy. Multiple instruments have been proposed by companies, national and international organizations, private associations, foundations, and non-governmental organizations (Organisation for Economic Co-operation and Development (OECD), 2001; European Commission, 2004).

In this chapter, we will first highlight the history of CSR and the reasons behind its various definitions. Following that, we present the ESG directives that have facilitated the adoption of more effective and transparent CSR strategies.

1.2 The Emergence of CSR and Its Definition

According to Pasquero (2005), the concept of CSR has a long history. It originated in the United States and spread geographically to reflect the new challenges of contemporary society. Social change has rendered it an indispensable concept, which is why it represents a new form of modernity in management. It is also a comprehensive paradigm whose richness can only be fully revealed through a historical recapitulation. This concept of CSR is known for its ambiguity and the multitude of interpretations it could have. Several versions coexist to explain its origins; it is common to see that several currents present themselves as founders of CSR as we know it today. To understand this concept, it is necessary to highlight the evolution of the CSR construct and to outline the logic of knowledge accumulation around the construct, which operates through semantic deposits, each referring to a specific stage of its theoretical development.

1.2.1 The History of CSR

1.2.1.1 The Philanthropic Origins of CSR: Christian Ethics and Social Institutions Before 1950

The origins of Corporate Social Responsibility (CSR) can be traced back to Roman law and English historical practices, which helped establish social institutions like hospitals and colleges, positioning companies as agents of social benefit. These organizations were seen both as economic entities and as serving the collective good. The company was considered a social and moral actor. As colonialism expanded, these ideas were carried over to the American colonies, supporting the notion of corporate social responsibility (Chaffee, 2017).

In the eighteenth and nineteenth centuries, Christian theology played a significant role in the evolution of CSR. Faced with poverty and poor working conditions, organizations like the YMCA (Young Men's Christian Association)[1], founded in 1844, applied Christian values to economic activities, influencing practices in the United States (Carroll, 2008; Heald, 1970). These philanthropic standards and principles, initially promoted by Christian associations and inspired by moral and theological principles, have gradually influenced private companies. For example, Macy's began collecting charitable donations as early as 1887, and the Pullman Palace Car Company built a model town in 1893 to improve the quality of life for its workers (Heald, 1970).

In the early twentieth century, CSR became more formal, and managers began integrating societal concerns into their goals. This shift in focus, initially driven by profit, now involves considering the interests of stakeholders, including workers and local communities. For example, the Pioneer Fund of 1928 avoided investing in companies with immoral practices, laying the groundwork for socially responsible investment (Carroll, 2008; Latapí Agudelo et al., 2019).

1.2.1.2 The Emergence of Modern CSR (1950–1980): Definitions, Theoretical Foundations, and Societal Expectations

The 1950s were a pivotal decade in the development of corporate social responsibility (CSR). During this period, researchers began to define CSR, emphasizing its theoretical foundations and practical applications. Lee (2008) states that the academic discussions of the 1950s and 1960s focused on the social level of analysis, laying the groundwork for applying CSR in practice (also connected to the goal of improving working conditions and reducing social inequalities by companies).

Following World War II, corporate philanthropy became a prevalent aspect of CSR practices, with firms engaging in limited activities beyond charitable contributions (Carroll, 2008). Howard Bowen's significant publication, *Social Responsibilities of the Businessman* (1953), is recognized as the first scholarly initiative to examine and define CSR. Bowen (1953)

[1] When George Williams founded the first YMCA in Industrial Revolution-era London, he sought to create a supportive community to help young men like himself address the pressing social challenges of the time (https://www.ymca.org).

contended that the increasing influence and power of many companies required the integration of social values into business decision-making processes. He highlights the crucial role of business leaders in incorporating these social values into their operations. His definition of Corporate Social Responsibility (CSR) as "*the obligations of businessmen to pursue those policies, to make those decisions, or to follow those lines of action which are desirable in terms of the objectives and values of our society*" (Bowen, 1953, p. 6) made him the "Father of Corporate Social Responsibility" (Carroll, 1999).

Following Bowen, numerous researchers have contributed to the growing body of knowledge on CSR. Eells (1956) expands on this idea by proposing a broader, more institutional conception of CSR. While Bowen focuses on the moral responsibility of managers, Eells views the company as a social institution, deeply rooted in a network of relationships with society. He emphasizes the growing complexity of social issues and the need for companies to respond to collective expectations, beyond individual morality alone. Eells makes CSR an organizational and systemic issue that goes beyond the ethical question. Selekman (1959) addressed the moral responsibility of management in response to workers' demands by incorporating the challenges of social dialogue. Davis (1960) developed the CSR discussion by associating social obligations with economic benefits. He calls for a proportional relationship between corporate behavior, in terms of economic power, and social responsibility. Similarly, Frederick (1960) differs from Bowen (1953) and Davis (1960) in proposing an evolutionary and societal conception of CSR. Whereas Bowen views it as a moral obligation that falls under the responsibility of individual managers, and Davis sees it as a strategic lever proportional to the power of companies, Frederick (1960) conceives of CSR as a regulatory function that balances economic dynamics and social expectations.

McGuire (1963) advocated for a broader definition of CSR that embraced political participation and community welfare. He proposed differentiating between economic, legal, and social responsibility, while Walton (1967) underlined the emerging ideological and legislative frameworks that positioned companies as essential contributors to social well-being. The socio-political upheavals of the late 1960s, including environmental and societal activism such as student struggles, feminist mobilization, and anti-Vietnam war demonstrations, resulted in a low level of public trust in the business world (Waterhouse, 2017), which was accused of neglecting the environment, concentrating too much economic power, or failing to take social demands sufficiently into account. Landmark incidents, such as the 1969 Santa Barbara oil spill, sparked a shift in public opinion toward corporate responsibility and drove governmental developments, including the founding of the Environmental Protection Agency (EPA) in 1970. These innovations represented a trend toward formalizing corporate responsibility in response to environmental and societal concerns and the beginning of a growing awareness of environmental issues.

The 1970s witnessed a significant broadening of the academic discourse around CSR. Whereas CSR was once seen as an obligation to be fulfilled by top management, it is now seen as a strategic element of corporate management. At the same time, it is the subject of academic research, with researchers attempting to analyze and understand the impact of CSR on corporate business strategy and decision-making processes in a managerial context. Carroll's (1979) pyramid of corporate social responsibility was a particularly influential contribution during this period, proposing a framework that categorized CSR into four components: economic, legal, ethical, and discretionary responsibilities. Similarly, the Committee for Economic Development (1971) enhanced the definition of CSR by publishing a report entitled "*The Social Responsibilities of Business Corporations.*" The report stated that companies exist by public permission and must therefore serve the needs of society. This approach supported the concept that CSR is not only a voluntary effort but also an essential part of a business's responsibility to maintain social confidence and legitimacy.

Despite the rising popularity of CSR, Friedman's (1970) critique of CSR as a diversion from a firm's primary mission to maximize shareholder value was supported by few economists. Friedman stated that social responsibility initiatives were an inefficient use of resources, detracting from the company's primary economic objective. His perspective highlighted the persistent contradiction between the economic and social objectives of companies.

1.2.1.3 The Operationalization of CSR (1980–2000): Models, Stakeholder Theory, and Environmental Paradigm Shifts

This period marked the strengthening of academic interest in frameworks, models, and methodologies for analyzing CSR from an operational perspective, rather than concentrating on its definitional construct (Carroll, 2008; Wankel, 2008). Jones (1980) was among the first to conceptualize CSR in a dynamic, operational approach. By insisting on the integration of social considerations in decision-making, his work paved the way for empirical and theoretical studies that sought to formalize, measure, and model this integration, like Tuzzolino and Armandi (1981) with their hierarchical framework to assess corporate performance and Strand (1983) with a systemic model that links organizational behavior to social responsibility. A significant theoretical advancement in this era was Freeman's (1984) seminal contribution, *Strategic Management: A Stakeholder Approach*, which laid the foundations for stakeholder theory. By redefining the firm as a constellation of relationships beyond shareholders alone, Freeman expanded the CSR discourse to incorporate the expectations, rights, and influences of all stakeholders in strategic management[2]. Concurrently, research has increasingly examined the impact of CSR on firms' overall performance, as illustrated by Cochran and Wood's (1984) study, which explored the relationship between CSR and financial performance using reputation indices. Wartick and Cochran (1985) further refined Carroll's (1979) framework by reorganizing it into principles, processes, and policies, thus advancing the integration of CSR into corporate governance structures.

During this decade, social concerns about environmental pollution, employee health, and safety gained more importance (Carroll, 2008). These challenges and key events, such as the founding of the World Commission on Environment and Development (1983) and the publishing of the Brundtland Commission's report Our Common Future (1987), created a rising international focus on sustainable development. Although not directly related to CSR, these events had an indirect impact on the concept of CSR, as they integrated business ethics and stakeholder management into business behavior. Hart (1995) emphasized that the unprecedented scale of environmental degradation, driven by exponential growth in industrial production, fossil fuel consumption, and population, poses systemic risks to ecological and human systems (Graedel & Crutzen, 1989; Schneider, 1989; Wilson, 1989). This recognition triggered a paradigm shift in strategic management towards pollution prevention, product stewardship, and sustainable development as emergent sources of competitive advantage. Such thinking laid the intellectual groundwork for integrating governance considerations alongside social and environmental dimensions in corporate strategies, eventually condensing into ESG frameworks during the 2000s.

[2] See also Chapter 3 for a detailed discussion of stakeholder theory.

1.2.1.4 Strategic Integration of CSR (2000–2010): From Compliance to Competitive Advantage

The beginning of the 2000s is considered a period of significant academic research, marked by the strategic integration of CSR with corporate management and managerial realities. Smith (2001) stated that CSR expanded beyond legal compliance to encompass companies' responsibility to a broader range of stakeholders, yielding long-term social benefits. Additionally, Lantos (2001) developed the notion of Strategic CSR (SCSR). He suggested that CSR becomes strategic when it aligns with profit-generation goals and focuses on activities that generate financial benefits, rather than adhering solely to the triple bottom line approach.

The 2000s also marked a turning point in the economic conceptualization of CSR, with increasing attention being paid to its strategic integration and alignment. Furthermore, the development of stakeholder theory has had a profound influence on managerial approaches to corporate social responsibility. Freeman (2001) and Friedman and Miles (2002) stated that companies must meet the changing needs of stakeholders, including suppliers, workers, consumers, and local communities. This method supported the idea that CSR is important to company governance and strategy. Marrewijk (2003) proposed a thorough analysis of CSR and Corporate Sustainability, showing varied levels of CSR integration within businesses. He viewed CSR as a strategic response to social concerns, with businesses adapting their structures and policies to align with growing societal responsibilities and expectations. His "five-tier" framework of Corporate Sustainability remains a reference point for understanding the different principles of CSR.

1.2.1.5 CSR in the Era of Shared Value Creation (2010–Present): Strategic CSR, CSV, and Sustainable Value Optimization

The concept of Corporate Social Responsibility (CSR) has undergone substantial changes, particularly in the 2010s, evolving from a focus on reputation management to a more strategic framework related to company operations. Porter and Kramer (2011) introduced the concept of Creating Shared Value (CSV) as a crucial step in redefining the purpose of companies. They contended that traditional CSR, which is generally focused on reputation development, misses a larger strategic integration essential for long-term success. CSV, in contrast, was described as "*policies and operating practices that enhance the competitiveness of a company while simultaneously advancing the economic and social conditions in the communities in which it operates*" (Porter & Kramer, 2011, p. 2). This method focused on identifying social requirements and aligning them with economic opportunities through three strategies: reevaluating goods and markets, redefining productivity within the value chain, and establishing a supportive industrial zone.

Porter and Kramer's work created a shift in how CSR was perceived, considering it as vital to building shared value rather than as a discretionary activity. Trapp (2012) elaborated on this notion by suggesting a "third generation" of CSR, where firms actively address social and global challenges through their operations, integrating these concerns with key business objectives. This indicates a greater acknowledgment of interconnectedness across the commercial, governmental, and social sectors, extending beyond Carroll's (1991) charitable obligations, which were previously considered voluntary and discretionary. Trapp demonstrated this transformation using Vattenfall's climate change campaign, which integrated social impact with strategic corporate objectives, illustrating a practical implementation of shared value creation.

The shift toward strategic CSR was further explored by Chandler and Werther (2013). They defined SCSR as "*the incorporation of a holistic CSR perspective within a firm's strategic planning and core operations so that the firm is managed in the interests of a broad set of stakeholders to achieve maximum economic and social value over the medium to long term*" (Chandler & Werther, 2013, p. 65). This notion reappears in Chandler's (2016) work, where value optimization is prioritized over profit maximization. Chandler (2016) highlighted five components of SCSR: incorporating CSR into strategic planning and company culture, aligning actions with core operations, adopting a stakeholder-responsive strategy, transitioning to medium- and long-term resource management, and optimizing value generation.

A crucial achievement in Chandler's approach was the focus on integrating CSR within corporate decision-making and culture, ensuring that CSR objectives are incorporated into day-to-day operations. By linking CSR programs with areas of expertise, corporations may change their focus from short-term profit to long-term shared value creation (Chandler, 2016). This approach reinforced the notion that sustainable value generation is not merely a strategic objective but also a fundamental obligation of modern organizations.

Carroll (2015) examined the evolution of CSR (Table 1.1), situating it within the broader context of related principles, including stakeholder

Table 1.1 Timeline of the evolution of CSR

Period	*Key Milestones and Concepts*
Before 1950	*Philanthropic Origins*: CSR rooted in Roman Law & English social institutions; Christian ethics shaping corporate charity (YMCA, Macy's donations, Pullman model town).
1950–1980	*Modern Definitions and Theoretical Foundations:* Bowen (1953): *Social Responsibilities of the Businessman*; Eells (1956), Selekman (1959), Davis (1960), Frederick (1960): moral responsibility, social contract, economic proportionality; McGuire (1963) expands to community welfare; Carroll's Pyramid (1979).
1980–2000	*Operationalization and Stakeholder Theory:* Jones (1980): dynamic operational approach; Cochran & Wood (1984): CSR & financial performance; Wartick & Cochran (1985): principles, processes, policies; Hart (1995): environmental paradigm shift and strategic implications.
2000–2010	*Strategic CSR:* Smith (2001): CSR beyond compliance; Lantos (2001): Strategic CSR (SCSR); Marrewijk (2003): CSR and Corporate Sustainability framework.
2010–Present	*Shared Value Creation & Sustainability Integration:*Porter & Kramer (2011): Creating Shared Value (CSV); Trapp (2012): Third-generation CSR; Chandler & Werther (2013), Chandler (2016): SCSR and value optimization; Carroll (2015): CSR, ethics, stakeholder engagement.

engagement, corporate citizenship, and business ethics. He recognized that these principles are interconnected and have together expanded the knowledge and practice of CSR. His research highlighted the integration of sustainability, ethics, and shared value within the CSR paradigm, underscoring its adaptability and applicability in addressing contemporary social concerns.

1.2.2 The Definition of CSR

Dejean and Gond (2004) argue that definitions of Corporate Social Responsibility (CSR) remain notably diverse, reflecting its conceptual ambiguity and evolving nature. They distinguish between academic definitions, rooted in theoretical frameworks and disciplinary perspectives, and institutional definitions, derived from policy documents and professional guidelines. This diversity in definitions is not merely a matter of semantics; it reflects the historical evolution of CSR itself. As highlighted in the previous section, each stage in the evolution of CSR from its philanthropic beginnings to its operational, strategic, and sustainability-focused forms has led to different interpretations shaped by the dominant socio-economic contexts, managerial paradigms, and stakeholder expectations.

The definitions presented in Table 1.2 demonstrate this ongoing conceptual growth. They highlight how CSR has shifted from being a moral and charitable duty to an operational element integrated into corporate governance, and more recently to a strategic necessity connected to sustainability and shared value creation. By presenting these key definitions in chronological order, we aim to clarify the intellectual history of CSR, showing that there is no single, universally agreed-upon definition of CSR. Instead, CSR is a complex and historically influenced concept whose meanings have evolved in response to shifting societal needs, theoretical advancements, and managerial practices. This variety of definitions remains a key aspect of current debates on CSR measurement, implementation, and integration into business models.

1.3 The Emergence of ESG Directives: From Ideation to Practice

In the previous section, we discussed the development of the CSR concept as outlined in existing academic literature. This development is driven by social movements and the regulations that define the rights and responsibilities of companies, but the academic literature also influences these regulations in return. In this section, we will examine the evolution of the ESG directives and guidelines.

1.3.1 The Early Stage of Voluntary Guidelines (1970s–1990s)

The 1970s reflect the incorporation of environmental and social factors into governing structures. In 1973, the European Community (EC) announced the initial Environmental Action Program (EAP). The program demonstrates a commitment to sustainable development, linking economic success with environmental stewardship. Simultaneously, the adoption of the Sullivan Principles in 1977 highlighted the importance of social equality in corporate governance. These principles, adapted from the Universal Declaration of Human Rights, aimed to address unfair labor practices in South Africa during the apartheid era. The Sullivan Principles aimed to integrate social responsibility into business operations and promote fair employment practices, reasonable salaries, and community

Table 1.2 Definitions of CSR: Academic and institutional perspectives

Type	*Author/Institution*	*Definition*
Academic	Bowen (1953)	"The obligations of businessmen to pursue those policies, to make those decisions, or to follow those lines of action which are desirable in terms of the objectives and values of our society."
Academic	Chamberlain (1953)	"Action that the leadership in business and unions are expected to take … as matters of right, whether legal or nonlegal."
Academic	Friedman (1962)	"There is one and only one social responsibility of business—to use its resources and engage in activities designed to increase its profits so long as it stays within the rules of the game."
Academic	McGuire (1963)	"Corporations have not only economic and statutory obligations but also certain responsibilities to society that extend beyond these obligations."
Academic	Backman (1975)	"CSR refers to the objectives or reasons that give a soul to business rather than the pursuit of economic performance."
Academic	Ackerman & Bauer (1976)	"Social responsibility means the obligation to take responsibility … Responsiveness enables firms to respond to social demand rather than decide unilaterally what to do."
Academic	Carroll (1979)	"CSR encompasses the economic, legal, ethical, and discretionary expectations that society has of organizations at any given time."
Academic	Jones (1980)	"Companies have obligations towards societal actors other than shareholders and beyond legal or contractual requirements."
Academic	Capra & Spretnak (1984)	"Social responsibility includes the economic domain, social justice, the social contract, social and civil rights, especially for women and minorities."
Academic	Wartick & Cochran (1985)	"Social responsibilities are determined by society. Firms must analyze expectations, develop accountability approaches, and implement appropriate responses to social problems."
Academic	Anderson (1986)	"CSR is exercised in three areas: legal compliance, moral and ethical standards, and philanthropic donations."
Academic	Wood (1991)	"Business and society are intertwined; society has expectations regarding corporate behavior and results."

Table 1.2 (continued)

Type	*Author/Institution*	*Definition*
Academic	Gond & Igalens (2003)	"CSR formalizes the idea that businesses, operating in social, political, and ecological environments, assume responsibilities beyond legal and economic obligations."
Academic	Capron & Quairel Lanoizelée (2004, 2007)	"CSR is the set of discourses and acts reflecting corporate attention to environmental and societal impacts, applying sustainable development values."
Academic	Pasquero (2005)	"All the obligations, legal or voluntary, a company assumes to be seen as a model of good citizenship."
Academic	Boidin (2008)	"CSR has a positive conception (engagement) and a normative conception (prescriptive actions, methods, benchmarks)."
Academic	Basu & Palazzo (2008)	"CSR materializes in managerial processes defining relationships with stakeholders, roles in the common good, and sustainable behaviors."
Institutional	Dow Jones Sustainability Index (1999)	"Internal CSR relates to corporate governance, risk and crisis management, codes of conduct/compliance/corruption and bribery, human capital development, and talent attraction and retention."
Institutional	Global Reporting Initiative (GRI) (2000)	"CSR practices guided by indicators such as employment, labor/management relations, occupational health and safety, diversity, equal opportunity, training, and education."
Institutional	EU GreenBook (2001)	"Being socially responsible means not only meeting legal obligations but also going beyond, investing more in human capital, the environment, and stakeholder relationships."
Institutional	World Bank (2004)	"CSR is the commitment to contribute to sustainable economic development by working with employees, families, communities, and society to improve quality of life, benefiting both development and business."
Institutional	European SMEs' Good Practice (2005)	"Internal CSR involves working conditions, job satisfaction, work/life balance, equal opportunities and diversity, training, staff development, employee communication, decision participation, and fair remuneration."
Institutional	ISO Normes 26000 (2010)	"Responsibility for impacts of decisions and activities on society and the environment through transparent and ethical behavior that contributes to sustainable development, considers stakeholder expectations, complies with laws, and is integrated throughout the organization."

well-being. Furthermore, the Third EAP (1982–1986) focused on standardizing emissions rules and adding environmental issues within the European Internal Market.

Concurrently, the 1987 report by the Brundtland Commission, Our Common Future, defined sustainable development as addressing "the needs of the present without compromising the ability of future generations to meet their own needs." This report created a worldwide conversation on the symbiotic link between economic development and environmental preservation, encouraging the incorporation of CSR concepts into global policy frameworks. In the 1970s and 1980s, as environmental issues emerged and remained a concern, the rules for environmental regulation were unclear, despite the intentions. At that time, there was no common legislative framework in Europe for all countries to reduce greenhouse gas emissions or water contamination. Some initiatives, such as the introduction of permits, were implemented but poorly monitored, and few companies were aware of them.

The Fourth Environmental Action Program (1987–1992) was a fundamental shift in the European Union's approach to environmental management. The program presented sectoral analysis and incorporated innovative tools such as taxes, subsidies, and tradable emission permits to address environmental issues. Additionally, the EU has positioned itself as a global leader in combating threats such as climate change by adopting long-term strategies and fostering international cooperation, particularly through the Kyoto Protocol. This period marked the increased integration of sustainability into economic and business activities, reflecting a shift from isolated environmental regulations to holistic frameworks that balance economic growth with social responsibility.

Building on this foundation, the Fifth Environmental Action Program (1992–1999) integrated crucial components from the Brundtland Report's conception of sustainable development. It introduced a sectoral strategy targeting high-pollution sectors such as transport, energy, and agriculture, shifting from end-of-pipe solutions towards structural improvements in production and consumption systems. The program promoted public transit, energy efficiency, and waste reduction, while employing market-oriented instruments such as fiscal incentives and voluntary agreements to engage both producers and consumers in environmental decision-making. Importantly, it recognized the pivotal role of non-governmental organizations and local governments in advocating environmental concerns, raising public awareness, and ensuring compliance with EU directives. These programs were implemented as instruments to drive environmental protection policies. The goal is to establish a regulatory framework that helps companies recognize their environmental impacts. Ultimately, they aimed to ensure that environmental objectives were systematically integrated into firms' strategic decisions and operational practices through dedicated reporting tools.

At the same time, the Global Reporting Initiative (GRI) was established in 1997 by CERES (formerly the Coalition for Environmentally Responsible Economies) in partnership with the United Nations Environment Program (UNEP) to standardize sustainability reporting globally. Its approach elevated sustainability disclosures to the level of financial reporting by emphasizing transparency, auditability, and stakeholder participation. These programs were implemented not only as voluntary reporting frameworks but also as tools to guide and implement environmental protection policies. Their primary goal was to help create regulatory frameworks that would increase corporate awareness of their environmental impacts. Ultimately, the aim was to ensure that environmental objectives were not just announced but genuinely integrated into companies' strategic decisions and operational practices through dedicated reporting tools.

In addition, France launched the Finansol label, guided by a committee of independent experts from civil society, to promote socially responsible investment by integrating ethical considerations into financial operations. Moreover, the Dow Jones Sustainability Index (DJSI), introduced in 1999, was the first ethical stock market index to provide investors with a baseline for evaluating business sustainability performance across economic, environmental, and social dimensions. The evaluation methodology of the DJSI is based on the obligations set by the GRI and the EAPs. It aligns its assessment criteria with internationally recognized sustainability reporting standards and regulatory environmental policies. This approach ensures that corporate performance benchmarks are comprehensive and comparable across all relevant areas of operation.

In addition to programs aimed at protecting the environment, other initiatives have emerged to encourage companies to adopt more socially responsible practices. The Governing Body of the International Labour Office agreed on the Tripartite Declaration of Principles concerning multinational companies and social policy at its 204th Session (November 1977). Subsequently, it updated it at its 279th Session (November 2000). The Tripartite Statement of Principles (MNE Statement) is the instrument that provides direct guidance to firms on social policy and inclusive, responsible, and sustainable workplace practices. The goal of this Declaration is to support the positive contribution that multinational firms may make to economic and social growth and the fulfillment of decent employment for all, and to minimize and resolve the challenges to which their different activities may give rise. Foreign and national firms, if the principles of the MNE Declaration are relevant to both, should be subject to the exact expectations in respect of their behavior in general and their social practices in particular. Companies in all countries are required to comply with health and safety standards that protect workers and respect their fundamental rights. This was not subject to reporting, but to the production of internal company documents demonstrating compliance with local laws (such as labor law, for example).

1.3.2 Formalization and the Rise of Reporting (2000s)

The 2000s marked a significant turning point in companies' reporting requirements. In 2001, France took a significant step with the Nouvelles Régulations Économiques (NRE) law, which required publicly listed firms to disclose the social and environmental impacts of their activities in their annual reports. Article 16 of this law established the initial legal requirement for non-financial reporting for 700 French-listed companies. This legislation was a groundbreaking move that encouraged companies to include non-financial factors in their investment decisions and promote corporate transparency. However, this law does not address voluntary commitments to sustainable development or human rights since there are no clear benchmarks for reporting, nor are there sanctions or mandatory third-party verifications in place.

That same year, the European Union reinforced its commitment to CSR with the release of the Green Paper on Corporate Social Responsibility. The paper promoted cooperation among authorities, companies, and other stakeholders to improve Corporate Social Responsibility (CSR).

Along with these legal achievements, the European Financial Reporting Advisory Group (EFRAG) was created in 2001 to represent European interests in shaping global accounting standards and to ensure alignment with the International Accounting Standards Board (IASB). At the same time, the European Sustainable Investment Forum (Eurosif) was established to promote socially responsible investment (SRI) across Europe. Eurosif's goals include encouraging best practices, influencing EU legislation, supporting its member organizations, and raising awareness about SRI.

Furthermore, global efforts to promote sustainability gained greater importance during the Johannesburg Earth Summit in 2002, where companies agreed on measures to preserve the global environment. Although these agreements were not legally required, they marked a shift in the company's perspective toward environmental responsibility. At the same time, the Sarbanes-Oxley Act in the United States introduced strict regulations to enhance corporate governance, financial reporting, and risk management. The law assigned individual accountability for financial disclosures, aiming to prevent fraud and corruption, and highlighted the broader movement toward ethics and accountability in business practices.

It was not until 2004 that the acronym ESG ("Environmental, Social, Governance") was formalized by a group of financial players under the auspices of the UN. This laid the foundations for sustainable finance, making ESG criteria a central element of corporate analysis and strategy. Subsequent years witnessed the approval of the Principles for Responsible Investment (2006) and the issuance of the first green bonds by the World Bank and the European Investment Bank (2007–2008), both of which underscored the financial sector's role in promoting sustainability. Meanwhile, Eurosif continued its advocacy on the issue of transparency guidelines in 2008, 2011, and 2013, providing guidance to asset management organizations on ESG integration and emphasizing the importance of transparent communication about ESG practices.

In France, the growth of the NRE law led to the adoption of the Grenelle II law (2010), which strengthened reporting obligations under Article 225. Beyond social and environmental impact disclosure, firms were now required to report on their societal commitments to sustainable development. This development in the NRE law reflected a deeper understanding of corporate accountability and an increased focus on sustainable development as a crucial part of company strategy. However, this legislation does not set any mandatory reporting standards. It also depends on large companies with over 500 employees, and there was no requirement to achieve results or face sanctions. Finally, the law also encouraged greenwashing. Companies issued reports detailing their environmental activities, but failed to follow through on their commitments.

1.3.3 Mandatory Reporting and Regional Regulations (2010s)

The 2010s witnessed significant legislative changes aimed at increasing accountability in corporate and regional governance, especially in response to environmental, social, and governance (ESG) concerns. These policies, both at the European and national levels, influenced the development of sustainable finance, corporate responsibility, and environmental protection.

In 2013, the European Union (EU) approved Directive 2013/34/EU, commonly known as the Accounting Directive. This directive aims to enhance the transparency and comparability of financial reports across member states, laying the groundwork for further standards in non-financial reporting. The Non-Financial Reporting Directive (NFRD) of 2014 (Directive 2014/95/EU) amended the 2013 directive, requiring large companies to disclose information on environmental, social, and employee issues, human rights, anti-corruption, and related topics. This change marked a significant step toward merging financial reporting with sustainability objectives. Simultaneously, national measures reinforced these goals. In France, the 2014 law on the Social and Solidarity Economy (ESS) aimed to promote economic activities that emphasize social benefits, solidarity, and regional development. This legislation supported groups balancing economic and social aims, fostering a more inclusive and sustainable economy.

The United Nations' adoption of the Sustainable Development Goals (SDGs) in 2015 further highlighted the global commitment to sustainability. In France, this vision was followed by the Energy Transition Law of 2015, which increased climate-related obligations for businesses and investors. This law aims to reduce dependence on nuclear energy, promote the use of renewable energy sources, enhance building energy efficiency, and encourage sustainable transportation practices. Supporting these initiatives, the French Ministry of Ecological Transition launched the Greenfin label in 2015, the first government-backed green finance label, which prohibited investments in nuclear and fossil fuel industries while encouraging green economic growth.

The United Kingdom's Modern Slavery Act (2015) set a global precedent by legally requiring companies with annual sales over £36 million to report on efforts to prevent modern slavery in their operations and supply chains. This law underscored the growing importance of incorporating human rights considerations into corporate governance. The French government significantly advanced sustainability with its 2015–2020 "Stratégie Nationale de Développement Durable" (SNDD), which built on its 2010–2013 predecessor. The strategy outlined a vision for a resilient society, supported by policies such as the Energy Transition for Green Growth Act (2015) and the 2019 Mobility Orientation Act, both of which emphasized low-carbon transitions and sustainable urban development.

Internationally, the 2016 adoption of the Paris Agreement by the UNFCCC (United Nations Framework Convention on Climate Change) upheld the global commitment to combating climate change. France supported this international pact through domestic policies, such as the Sapin II Law (2016), which introduced strict anti-corruption measures, and the Responsible Investment Label (RIL), promoting socially responsible investment practices.

In 2017, France took a significant step by passing the Corporate Duty of Vigilance Law, which requires large companies to monitor environmental, social, and governance risks throughout their entire supply chains. This regulation highlighted the growing need for companies to adhere to ESG principles not only internally but also in their external operations. At the same time, the Bank of France established the Network for Greening the Financial System (NGFS) to unite central banks and financial regulators in pursuit of sustainability goals. Building on these efforts, France introduced the Circular Economy Roadmap (2018), aiming for a 30% reduction in resource use by 2030, a 25% decrease in non-hazardous waste by 2025, and a 100% recycling rate for plastics by that year. These initiatives aim to guide France toward a more sustainable and resource-efficient economy.

At the European level, the adoption of the Green Loan Principles (GLP) and the European Taxonomy in 2018 provided a framework for sustainable investments, defining what constitutes ecologically sustainable economic activity. In 2019, the French PACTE (Action plan for business growth and transformation) Law strengthened sustainability in corporate governance by requiring companies to address social and environmental challenges, declare a purpose beyond profit, and adopt a "mission-driven" status if desired. The result of these efforts was the European Green Deal (2019), a groundbreaking strategy aimed at achieving net-zero greenhouse gas emissions by 2050, decoupling economic growth from resource use, and ensuring a fair transition. France supported this initiative with the Grenelle II Law, which promotes energy savings, renewable energy sources, and reductions in greenhouse gas emissions. These developments throughout the 2010s demonstrate the integration of mandated reporting and regional directives into broader sustainability goals, reflecting a growing consensus on the importance of corporate responsibility and sustainable development. This period laid the groundwork for a new wave of legislative progress, placing ESG principles at the center of economic and financial governance.

1.3.4 Harmonization and ESG Integration (2020s–Present)

The 2020s marked a crucial period in global sustainability efforts, driven by ambitious legislative initiatives and a rising awareness of environmental, social, and governance (ESG) priorities. The European Green Deal, launched in 2020, established the essential framework for reaching decarbonization by 2050. A significant outcome of this effort was the EU Taxonomy Regulation (Regulation (EU) 2020/852), which established a standardized system for categorizing sustainable economic activities. This legislative framework is intended to direct capital toward sustainable projects, ensuring alignment with primary environmental goals, including climate change mitigation and adaptation.

The COVID-19 pandemic further highlighted the importance of resilience and sustainability in economic and financial institutions. ESG funds showed notable resilience during the crisis, a trend also seen during the 2008 financial crisis. Three main factors supported this resilience: (1) a pandemic-resistant asset allocation focusing on sectors like healthcare and social services, (2) a shift from traditional market dynamics with ESG assets maintaining long-term stability despite lower short-term trading volumes, and (3) the commitment of ESG investors, who prioritized long-term value over immediate financial returns.

The pandemic's monetary policy also affected financial markets. Governments acquired substantial debt to support their economies, with central banks enabling these actions, thereby stimulating market activity. Additionally, the crisis increased environmental awareness, emphasizing the importance of green investments. Notably, one-third of the EU's €750 billion recovery plan in 2020 was allocated to funding green bonds, demonstrating a strong commitment to accelerating the green transition. The epidemic also highlighted the importance of social factors in economic activities. Issues such as worker health, remote work, and partial unemployment have gained unprecedented attention, prompting governments to incorporate social considerations into their sustainability strategies. This time witnessed requests for a standardized social taxonomy similar to the EU Taxonomy for environmental goals, aiming to standardize social impact assessments and reporting.

Transparency became a key topic during this period, with regulatory changes focusing on the financial sector's reporting responsibilities. The Sustainable Finance Disclosure Regulation (SFDR), introduced in 2021, improved the EU Taxonomy by requiring financial firms to disclose ESG-related information about their products. The SFDR classifies financial products into three groups (Article 6, Article 8, and Article 9) based on how they address ESG factors, with Article 9 products being the most committed to meeting sustainability goals. The SFDR's dual-materiality approach obliges firms to report both how sustainability risks impact investment value and the negative externalities investments may have on sustainability indicators.

In parallel, the Corporate Sustainability Reporting Directive (CSRD), approved in 2022, aimed to unify sustainability reporting among European companies. Building on the Non-Financial Reporting Directive (NFRD), the CSRD expanded its scope to include a broader range of firms, excluding microenterprises, and established specific reporting requirements based on the European Sustainability Reporting Standards (ESRS). These guidelines covered universal, sector-specific, and SME-focused rules, providing comprehensive and transparent sustainability disclosures. To implement the CSRD, the European Financial Reporting Advisory Group (EFRAG) was tasked with developing the ESRS. The regulation also mandated the use of digital reporting formats and required external validation of the submitted information, thereby improving data reliability and accessibility. These measures are gradually being rolled out, with full compliance expected by 2024. The alignment between the EU Taxonomy and the SFDR significantly strengthened the regulatory framework. While the Taxonomy defined what constitutes sustainable economic activity, the SFDR ensured transparency in the financial sector, enabling investors to make informed decisions aligned with their sustainability goals. Together, these guidelines underscore the EU's commitment to fostering long-term investments that support sustainable development.

Other notable developments during this period included the French Tech "Green20" program in 2023, which supported innovative startups in advancing green technologies, and the Corporate Sustainability Due Diligence Directive (CSDD), established to take effect in 2024, which aimed to incorporate sustainability considerations into corporate governance practices.

1.4 Conclusion

This chapter has explored the conceptual and historical foundations of CSR. Firstly, we trace its evolution from philanthropic and ethical concerns to a strategic, governance-centered approach embodied in ESG practices. Through an examination of key intellectual milestones, we have illustrated how CSR has responded to shifting societal expectations, environmental crises, and academic debates. The multiplicity of definitions across time highlights both the richness and ambiguity of the concept, reflecting the ideological and institutional contexts in which it has evolved.

Secondly, we highlighted that the emergence of ESG directives has played a decisive role in shaping and standardizing corporate sustainability practices. From voluntary guidelines to binding regulatory frameworks, ESG norms have increasingly translated CSR principles into measurable and reportable obligations. These directives, originating from national, international organizations, and market institutions, have contributed to the operationalization of CSR.

By bridging theoretical evolution with institutional practice, this chapter lays the groundwork for understanding how ESG has emerged not merely as an extension of CSR but as a transformative framework redefining corporate responsibility in the twenty-first century. The following chapters will delve deeper into the mechanisms, performance implications, and business model transformations associated with the integration of ESG.

References

Ackerman, R. W., & Bauer, R. A. (1976). *Corporate social responsiveness*. Reston Publishing.

Anderson, J. W. (1986). Social responsibility and the corporation. *Business Horizons, 29*(4), 22–27. https://doi.org/10.1016/0007-6813(86)90019-4

Backman, J. (Ed.). (1975). *Social responsibility and accountability*. New York University Press.

Basu, K., & Palazzo, G. (2008). Corporate social responsibility: A process model of sensemaking. *Academy of Management Review, 33*(1), 122–136.

Boidin, B. (2008). Introduction: Les enjeux de la responsabilité sociale et environnementale des entreprises dans les pays en développement. Monde en Développement, (4), 7–12.

Bowen, H. R. (1953). *Social responsibilities of the businessman*. University of Iowa Press.

Capra, F., & Spretnak, C. (1984). Green politics. *National Forum, 64*(3), 21.

Capron, M., & Quairel-Lanoizelée, F. (2004). *Mythes et réalités de l'entreprise responsable: Acteurs, enjeux, stratégie*. La Découverte.

Capron, M., & Quairel-Lanoizelée, F. (2007). *La responsabilité sociale des entreprises*. La Découverte.

Carroll, A. B. (1979). A three-dimensional conceptual model of corporate performance. *Academy of Management Review, 4*(4), 497–505.

Carroll, A. B. (1991). The pyramid of corporate social responsibility: Toward the moral management of organizational stakeholders. *Business Horizons, 34*(4), 39–48.

Carroll, A. B. (1999). Corporate social responsibility. *Business & Society, 38*(3), 268–295.

Carroll, A. B. (2008). A history of corporate social responsibility: Concepts and practices. In *A. Crane, D. Matten, J. Moon, & D. Siegel (Eds.), The Oxford handbook of corporate social responsibility* (pp. 19–46). Oxford University Press.

Carroll, A. B. (2015). Corporate social responsibility: The centerpiece of competing and complementary frameworks. *Organizational Dynamics, 44*(2), 87–96.

Chaffee, E. C. (2017). The origins of corporate social responsibility. *University of Cincinnati Law Review, 85*, 347–373.

Chamberlain, N. W. (1953). *Social responsibility and stripes.* Harper & Row.

Chandler, D. (2016). *Strategic corporate social responsibility: Sustainable value creation.* SAGE Publications.

Chandler, D., & Werther, W. B. (2013). *Strategic corporate social responsibility: Stakeholders, globalization, and sustainable value creation* (3rd ed.). SAGE Publications.

Cochran, P. L., & Wood, R. A. (1984). Corporate social responsibility and financial performance. *Academy of Management Journal, 27*(1), 42–56.

Davis, K. (1960). Can business afford to ignore social responsibilities? *California Management Review, 2*(3), 70–76.

Dejean, F., & Gond, J.-P. (2004). Responsabilité sociétale de l'entreprise: Enjeux stratégiques et méthodologies de recherche. *Finance Contrôle Stratégie, 57*(6), 741–764.

Eells, R. S. F. (1956). *Corporation giving in a free society.* Harper.

Frederick, W. C. (1960). The growing concern over business responsibility. *California Management Review, 2*(4), 54–61.

Freeman, R. E. (2001). A stakeholder theory of the modern corporation. *Perspectives in Business Ethics, 3*, 144.

Friedman, A. L., & Miles, S. (2002). Developing stakeholder theory. *Journal of Management Studies, 39*(1), 1–21.

Friedman, M. (1962). *Capitalism and freedom.* University of Chicago Press.

Friedman, M. (1970, September 13). The social responsibility of business is to increase its profits. *The New York Times Magazine.*

Gond, J.-P., & Igalens, J. (2003). La mesure de la performance sociale de l'entreprise: Une analyse critique et empirique des données ARESE. *Revue de Gestion des Ressources Humaines, 50*, 111–130.

Graedel, T. E., & Crutzen, P. J. (1989). The changing atmosphere. *Scientific American, 261*(3), 58–69.

Hart, S. L. (1995). A natural-resource-based view of the firm. *Academy of Management Review, 20*(4), 986–1014. https://doi.org/10.2307/258963

Heald, M. (1970). *The social responsibilities of business: Company and community 1900–1960.* Case Western Reserve University Press.

Jones, T. M. (1980). Corporate social responsibility revisited, redefined. *California Management Review, 22*(3), 59–67.

Lantos, G. P. (2001). The boundaries of strategic corporate social responsibility. *Journal of Consumer Marketing, 18*(7), 595–632.

Latapí Agudelo, M. A., Jóhannsdóttir, L., & Davídsdóttir, B. (2019). A literature review of the history and evolution of corporate social responsibility. *International Journal of Corporate Social Responsibility, 4*(1), 1–23.

Lee, M.-D. P. (2008). A review of the theories of corporate social responsibility: Its evolutionary path and the road ahead. *International Journal of Management Reviews, 10*(1), 53–73.

Marrewijk, M. (2003). Concepts and definitions of CSR and corporate sustainability: Between agency and communion. *Journal of Business Ethics, 44*, 95–105.

McGuire, J. W. (1963). *Business and society.* McGraw-Hill.

Pasquero, J. (2005). La responsabilité sociale de l'entreprise comme objet des sciences de gestion: Un regard historique. In *M.-F. Turcotte & A. Salmon (Eds.), Responsabilité sociale et environnementale de l'entreprise* (pp. 80–111). Presses de l'Université du Québec.

Pasquero, J. (2005). La responsabilité sociale de l'entreprise comme objet des sciences de gestion: Le concept et sa portée. In *M.-F. Turcotte & A. Salmon (Eds.), Responsabilité sociale et environnementale de l'entreprise* (pp. 112–143). Presses de l'Université du Québec.

Porter, M. E., & Kramer, M. R. (2011). Creating shared value. *Harvard Business Review.*

Schneider, S. H. (1989). The changing climate. *Scientific American, 261*(3), 70–79.

Selekman, B. M. (1959). *A moral philosophy for management.* McGraw-Hill.

Smith, N. C. (2001). Changes in corporate practices in response to public interest advocacy and actions. In *P. N. Bloom & G. T. Gundlach (Eds.), Handbook of marketing and society.* SAGE Publications.

Strand, R. (1983). A systems paradigm of organizational adaptations to the social environment. *Academy of Management Review, 8*(1), 90–96.

Trapp, N. L. (2012). Corporation as climate ambassador: Transcending business sector boundaries in a Swedish CSR campaign. *Public Relations Review, 38*(3), 458–465.

Tuzzolino, F., & Armandi, B. R. (1981). A need-hierarchy framework for assessing corporate social responsibility. *Academy of Management Review, 6*(1), 21–28.

Walton, C. C. (1967). *Corporate social responsibilities.* Wadsworth Publishing Company.

Wankel, C. (2008). *21st century management: A reference handbook.* SAGE Publications.

Wartick, S. L., & Cochran, P. L. (1985). The evolution of the corporate social performance model. *Academy of Management Review, 10*(4), 758–769.

Waterhouse, B. C. (2017). The personal, the political and the profitable: Business and protest culture, 1960s–1980s. Financial History, Spring, 14–17.
Wilson, E. O. (1989). Threats to biodiversity. *Scientific American, 261*(3), 108–117.
Wood, D. J. (1991). Corporate social performance revisited. *Academy of Management Review, 16*(4), 691–718.

CHAPTER 2

Non-Financial Reporting: Challenges and Implications for Investors

Hélène Ostrowski, Wissal Zribi, Jean-Claude Brou, and Nejwa Al-Alami

Abstract This chapter delves into the evolving non-financial reporting landscape in the European financial sector, emphasizing the strategic and regulatory shifts driven by ESG imperatives. The first section presents the EU's regulatory response to greenwashing and the demand for greater transparency by developing a harmonized sustainable finance framework. The EU Taxonomy and the Sustainable Finance Disclosure Regulation (SFDR) are central to this framework, which provides a structured classification of sustainable economic activities and imposes transparency obligations on financial market participants. The chapter elucidates how these instruments enhance investor confidence and facilitate capital allocation that is aligned with long-term sustainability objectives.

H. Ostrowski
Autonomie et Solidarité (A&S), Lille, France

W. Zribi • N. Al-Alami
ICL, Junia, Université Catholique de Lille, LITL

J.-C. Brou (✉)
ESG Finance, Courbevoie, France
e-mail: k.brou@esgf.com

S. Kendo (ed.), *Non-Financial Reporting and ESG Performance*,
Palgrave Studies in Impact Finance,
https://doi.org/10.1007/978-3-032-19092-5_2

The second section addresses the integration of ESG reporting into financial decision-making and its inherent challenges. It contrasts the standardized, audit-driven nature of financial reporting with the fragmented, voluntary frameworks of ESG disclosures. Drawing on empirical findings of previous academic research, it highlights issues such as selective disclosure, greenwashing, a lack of standardized indicators, particularly for SMEs, and the informational asymmetry investors face. The chapter ultimately underscores the need for more robust, comparable, and transparent ESG reporting standards to support meaningful investment decisions and sustainable development outcomes.

Keywords EU taxonomy • SFDR • Sustainable Finance • ESG

2.1 Introduction

The need for increased compliance in the European financial sector stems from several legislative and regulatory initiatives aimed at addressing environmental, social, and governance (ESG) challenges while ensuring transparency and sustainability in investment practices. This evolving regulatory landscape signals a fundamental transformation in financial governance, where the integration of ESG principles has moved from a voluntary commitment to a binding and structural requirement. Recognizing the urgency of climate issues and global sustainability objectives, the European Union (EU) has established a legislative framework that aligns financial practices with the United Nations' Sustainable Development Goals (SDGs) and the Paris Agreement.

This framework aims to address several key issues. Firstly, it combats greenwashing, a phenomenon that emerged with the rise of investments labeled as "sustainable," wherein some companies or funds presented themselves as more environmentally responsible than they truly were. To address this, a series of binding instruments such as the Sustainable Finance Disclosure Regulation (SFDR), the Taxonomy Regulation, and the Corporate Sustainability Reporting Directive (CSRD) has been introduced to define clear criteria and impose disclosure obligations on financial actors, thereby ensuring that only genuinely sustainable financial products can bear such designations and strengthening market credibility while minimizing the risks of misleading claims.

Secondly, the framework establishes a European Single Market for Sustainable Finance, driven by instruments such as the EU Taxonomy and other key disclosure regulations. These instruments standardize ESG data communication, creating a transparent and consistent environment that guides investor decisions, boosts investor confidence, and provides stability for responsible investments. Furthermore, the CSRD expands ESG reporting obligations to a broader range of companies, reinforcing comparability and data quality across the EU.

Thirdly, the EU has established rigorous transparency and accountability regulations, compelling financial entities, such as asset managers and investment funds, to disclose detailed non-financial information regarding the environmental and social impacts of their investments. This ensures enhanced transparency in risk management and encourages systematic integration of ESG considerations into investment strategies. The Corporate Sustainability Due Diligence Directive (CSDDD) further strengthens this dynamic by imposing a duty of care on companies across their entire value chain, especially regarding human rights and environmental risks.

Additionally, the EU's ESG regulations are increasingly aligned with international standards, such as those set by the Task Force on Climate-related Financial Disclosures (TCFD), the Global Reporting Initiative (GRI), and the Sustainability Accounting Standards Board (SASB). More recently, the integration of the International Sustainability Standards Board's (ISSB) International Financial Reporting Standards (IFRS) Sustainability Disclosure Standards has enhanced the interoperability of ESG reporting across jurisdictions. Such convergence enhances the global comparability of ESG data, allowing investors to effectively benchmark sustainability practices worldwide and integrate sustainable finance into the broader global financial system.

Ultimately, the framework addresses the growing demand from institutional investors, including pension funds and asset managers, who are increasingly requiring detailed ESG disclosures to mitigate long-term portfolio risks. Consequently, financial actors must adhere to the EU's rigorous ESG standards to satisfy this investor demand and attract sustainability-focused investments.

Taken together, these various legislative and regulatory initiatives at both national and European levels form a comprehensive architecture for sustainable finance, aiming to reconcile financial performance with long-term environmental and social objectives.

This book chapter is structured around two main sections. The first section focuses on compliance imperatives by presenting the European regulatory framework for sustainable finance, particularly the EU Taxonomy and the SFDR, and their implications for investors. The second section highlights various research and market perspectives on integrating ESG criteria into the financial sphere, emphasizing the challenges and strategic considerations that investors face in aligning financial performance with sustainability objectives.

2.2 Compliance Imperatives: The European Taxonomy, SFDR, and Regulatory Framework for Sustainable Finance

The European financial sector's need for compliance with sustainability regulations primarily aims to reduce ESG risks and ensure transparency, thereby guiding investments towards genuine sustainability. In this context, the European Taxonomy and the SFDR provide structured frameworks essential for aligning investment practices with environmental and social objectives. By establishing clear definitions, classification criteria, and disclosure requirements, these instruments help combat greenwashing and promote consistency in ESG reporting. The following sections specifically examine how these regulatory instruments affect investors and promote European sustainable investment practices. They also shed light on the operational and strategic challenges faced by financial actors in adapting to this evolving compliance landscape.

2.2.1 *The European Taxonomy: Classification of Sustainable Activities*

The EU Green Taxonomy is a classification system for economic activities that identifies those considered environmentally sustainable, as they neither contribute to climate change nor exacerbate environmental degradation. Described as an accurate "environmental compass" for the European Union, the Taxonomy was launched by the European Commission in 2018 to guide and mobilize private investment toward achieving climate neutrality by 2050. It forms a core component of the EU's Sustainable Finance Strategy and is rooted in Regulation (EU) 2020/852. This initiative aims to direct financial resources toward projects and activities that positively contribute to environmental sustainability, while mitigating the risks associated with greenwashing. It also provides a harmonized framework for financial actors, policymakers, and companies to assess the sustainability of economic activities across sectors.

An activity must satisfy three strict cumulative conditions to be classified as "sustainable" and aligned with the EU Taxonomy.

First, the activity must significantly contribute positively to one of the six environmental objectives defined by the Taxonomy:

1. Climate change mitigation,
2. Climate change adaptation,
3. Sustainable use and protection of water and marine resources,
4. Transition to a circular economy (including waste reduction and resource reuse),
5. Pollution prevention, and
6. Protection and restoration of biodiversity and ecosystems.

This means the activity must contribute in a measurable and meaningful way to achieving the environmental sustainability goals set at the European level. For instance, a company producing renewable energy would significantly reduce greenhouse gas emissions and mitigate climate change. The criteria for substantial contribution are further detailed in delegated acts issued by the European Commission, which include science-based thresholds and performance benchmarks.

Second, in addition to positively contributing to one objective, the activity must not significantly harm any of the remaining five environmental objectives. This condition prevents counterproductive or harmful solutions that may undermine sustainability, for example, exploiting natural resources at the expense of biodiversity or adopting industrial practices that, while reducing CO_2 emissions, cause significant pollution or damage fragile ecosystems. An activity that reduces carbon emissions but results in large-scale deforestation would not be considered Taxonomy-aligned, as it would negatively impact biodiversity. This requirement reflects the "Do No Significant Harm" (DNSH) principle, which is central to the EU's sustainability assessment.

Third, the activity must comply with fundamental human rights, decent working conditions, and minimum social standards. The Taxonomy stipulates that sustainable economic activities must consider not only environmental impact but also social responsibility, ensuring respect for the rights of workers and local communities. For example, a company engaging in forced labor or failing to uphold basic workplace safety standards would not meet the Taxonomy's requirements, even if it made progress in environmental sustainability. These social safeguards are aligned with international frameworks such as the OECD (Organisation for Economic Co-operation and Development) Guidelines for Multinational Enterprises and the UN Guiding Principles on Business and Human Rights.

Additionally, under the CSRD, large companies and financial institutions are required to disclose the proportion of their turnover, capital expenditure (CapEx), and operating expenditure (OpEx) that is aligned with the Taxonomy. This enhances transparency and facilitates a better assessment of the sustainability performance of economic actors by investors.

Examining concrete examples from various sectors can help us better understand how the EU taxonomy is applied in practice:

- In the renewable energy sector, solar, wind, or hydroelectric power projects are considered sustainable under the Taxonomy. These activities actively contribute to reducing CO_2 emissions and comply with other environmental criteria while avoiding natural resource degradation.
- In the transport sector, electric vehicles, low-emission public transport infrastructure, and sustainable mobility technologies align with the Taxonomy if they do not cause pollution or other significant environmental harm.
- In the building and construction sector, projects involving energy-efficient buildings and the use of environmentally friendly materials are considered taxonomy-compliant. However, compliance is conditional upon these projects not harming other environmental objectives and adhering to social and safety standards for workers.

The primary objective of the EU Green Taxonomy is to establish a clear and consistent standard for identifying genuinely environmentally sustainable activities, thereby guiding long-term investments toward projects that support the transition to a sustainable and carbon-neutral economy. By creating a standard classification system, the Taxonomy improves the comparability and reliability of ESG data across the EU. It ensures that investments meet rigorous sustainability criteria, thereby strengthening investor confidence. Ultimately, this initiative aims to channel financial flows into activities that contribute to the energy transition, climate resilience, and respect for social standards, thereby promoting a more sustainable and responsible European economy. It also contributes to the EU's broader objective of aligning capital markets with the European Green Deal and the Paris Agreement.

2.2.2 The SFDR: Transparency Obligations for Financial Actors

In the European Union, the SFDR, in force since March 2021, aims to strengthen transparency among financial market participants regarding sustainable finance and to combat greenwashing by introducing harmonized reporting standards. The regulation imposes disclosure obligations on asset managers, investment funds, providers of insurance-based investment products, and, more broadly, financial institutions, requiring them to publish annual non-financial data on the assets they manage, particularly with respect to environmental, social, and governance (ESG) criteria.

The regulation covers a wide range of financial products, whether or not they are labeled “green”: investment funds, life insurance products, retirement solutions, managed portfolios, securitization instruments, and certain structured or derivative products. The central objective is to make the ESG positioning of each product clear through a standardized classification, which distinguishes between products without ESG commitments (Article 6), those that promote environmental or social characteristics (Article 8), and those that pursue an explicit sustainable investment objective (Article 9). This categorization must be included in pre-contractual and periodic documents to ensure comparability and transparency for investors.

The implementation of the SFDR has profoundly transformed transparency requirements in European finance. It requires entities to describe their ESG risk integration policy and explain how these factors influence their investment decisions, while also disclosing potential adverse impacts (PAIs, Principal Adverse Impacts). At the product level, the standardized classification and mandatory inclusion of this information in pre-contractual and periodic documents provide investors with a transparent and comparable view of sustainability commitments. This increased transparency aims to reduce greenwashing, strengthen trust, and direct capital towards activities aligned with the European Union’s climate and social objectives.

2.2.2.1 SFDR 2.0 Developments (Proposal of November 21, 2025)

Recognizing the limitations of the initial framework, the European Commission presented an ambitious reform to simplify and clarify it.

SFDR 2.0 abandons the classification by Articles 6, 8, and 9 in favor of three new categories: Transition, ESG Basics, and Sustainable (Table 2.1). Each category has a minimum threshold of 70% of aligned assets and mandatory exclusions (controversial weapons, tobacco, OECD/UN violations, with strengthened fossil fuel restrictions for the Sustainable category). The reform introduces a normative definition of impact investing, eliminates entity-level PAI reporting obligations while strengthening product-level criteria, and mandates a highly standardized two-page report integrated into pre-contractual and periodic documents. It also removes the SFDR product sheet from websites and excludes investment advice and discretionary portfolio management from the scope.

From a comparability perspective (Table 2.2), reporting obligations will henceforth be concentrated on financial products subject to harmonized criteria and mandatory exclusion rules. The revised regulation is intended to be exclusionary, standardized, harmonized, and incentive-based for sectors and/or activities undergoing transition. These changes aim to improve readability for investors, reduce compliance costs, and strengthen the fight against greenwashing.

The new regulation is expected to come into force no earlier than 2028, following the adoption of delegated acts and technical standards. More than just a reporting tool, the SFDR is emerging as a strategic lever for redirecting financial flows towards the ecological and social transition, in line with the European Green Deal.

Table 2.1 Comparative summary SFDR 2021 and the new SFDR 2.0 due to 2028

Criteria	*SFDR 1.0 (Articles 6/8/9)*	*SFDR 2.0 (Transition/ESG Basics/Sustainable)*
Classification	*Article 6/8/9.*	*Transition/ESG Basics/Sustainable.*
Minimum threshold	*Not defined.*	*≥ 70% of aligned assets.*
Exclusions	*Not harmonized.*	*Mandatory baseline + fossil fuel restrictions.*
Impact investing	*Not defined.*	*Recognized and regulated.*
PAIs (principal adverse impacts)	*Mandatory at entity and product level.*	*Removed at entity level, maintained at product level.*
Reporting	*Detailed annexes + website disclosure.*	*Standardized format ≤ 2 pages, website disclosure removed.*
Scope	*Includes advisory services and mandates.*	*Excluded from the scope of SFDR.*

Table 2.2 Comparative summary of fund classifications under the SFDR (new classification)

Criteria	*Transition (Art. 7)*	*ESG Basics (Art. 8)*	*Sustainable (Art. 9)*
Consideration of ESG criteria	*Mandatory (credible transition strategy).*	*Mandatory (systematic integration of ESG factors).*	*Mandatory (explicit sustainability objective).*
Type of investment	*Assets contributing to the transition (credible plans, active engagement).*	*Assets with high ESG ratings, strong ESG practices.*	*Sustainable assets aligned with the Taxonomy, green bonds, Paris Agreement-aligned indices.*
Minimum threshold	*≥ 70% of assets aligned with the transition strategy.*	*≥ 70% of assets integrating ESG criteria.*	*≥ 70% of sustainable investments.*
Mandatory exclusions	*Controversial weapons, tobacco, OECD/UN violations.*	*Mandatory exclusion baseline.*	*Baseline + reinforced fossil fuel exclusions.*
Fossil fuels	*Allowed under conditions (credible transition).*	*Allowed under conditions.*	*Prohibited.*
Transparency requirements	*Standardized reporting ≤ 2 pages (pre-contractual + periodic).*		
Governance requirement	*Good governance required.*		
Alignment with SDGs / OECD	*Recommended.*		*Mandatory.*
Anti-greenwashing controls	*Increased monitoring.*		*Strictest requirements.*
Expected impact	*Measurable contribution to the transition.*	*ESG improvement without strict impact objective.*	*Clear objective of measurable sustainable impact (e.g., CO_2 reduction, social inclusion).*

2.2.3 Sustainable Finance in France: Key Dynamics and Recent Developments

In France, sustainable finance comprises three main approaches: responsible, solidarity-based, and green finance. Each of these dimensions aims to address significant economic and social challenges by directing capital flows toward projects that have a positive and lasting impact on society and the environment. Financial actors rely on ESG (Environmental,

Social, and Governance) criteria to guide their investments toward sustainable activities that align with long-term societal goals. France has played a pioneering role in this area, notably through Article 173 of the 2015 Energy Transition Law, which was one of the first legislative texts in the world to require institutional investors to disclose how they integrate climate-related and ESG risks into their strategies.

To ensure accountability and demonstrate the integrity of funds labeled as "sustainable," various labeling schemes have been created to certify compliance with specific sustainability standards. These labels, such as ISR (Socially Responsible Investment), Greenfin, and Finansol, serve as both tools to guide investors and measures to combat greenwashing. While labels help increase market transparency and boost investor confidence, their role has been extensively discussed in Chapter 1. It is essential to note that these national schemes complement European regulatory frameworks, such as the SFDR and the EU Taxonomy, by introducing additional requirements, particularly regarding sector exclusions and measurable environmental impacts.

Regarding market size, the "*Association française de la gestion financière*" (AFG) reports that by 2023, 1,037 funds managed in France held at least one sustainability label, with total assets under management amounting to €805 billion. Among these funds, 85% were certified under the ISR label, while 2.2% carried the Greenfin label and 1% the Finansol label. Additionally, 279 funds were certified under non-French European labels, representing €220 billion, or 27% of all labeled investment funds. These included the Towards Sustainability label (85%), the FNG-Siegel (10%), and the LuxFLAG ESG (9%). This strong uptake illustrates the dynamism of the French sustainable finance market, which remains one of the most mature in Europe. The broad adoption of the ISR label, despite criticisms over its lack of stringency, reflects a broad commitment across the industry to formalize ESG integration practices.

French financial regulators, particularly the AMF and the ACPR (Autorité de Contrôle Prudentiel et de Résolution), play an increasingly active role in monitoring ESG claims, promoting transparency, and aligning national practices with EU regulations. The AMF has published detailed guidance to restrict the use of sustainability-related terminology in fund marketing and communications, aiming to prevent greenwashing and ensure consistency with SFDR classifications.

France has also positioned itself as a leading voice in Europe for integrating climate and biodiversity-related risks into financial supervision.

Stress tests carried out by the ACPR now incorporate climate scenarios, and the government has expressed support for expanding ESG reporting to include biodiversity impacts. These developments reflect a growing ambition to move beyond carbon metrics toward a broader understanding of sustainability risks and impacts.

Finally, despite significant progress, challenges remain. These include the heterogeneity of ESG methodologies, the limited availability of high-quality non-financial data, particularly from SMEs, and the ongoing tension between voluntary commitments and regulatory compliance. Maintaining investor trust will require continuous efforts to enhance data reliability, harmonize frameworks, and measure the real-world outcomes of so-called "sustainable" investments.

2.2.4 Responsible Investment Trends in France: Focus on AFG Reporting

According to the 2023 report by the AFG, assets under management (AUM) in responsible investment (RI) in France reached €2,531 billion by the end of 2023 under the SFDR framework, marking a 5.8% increase compared to 2022. The report highlights that French investment funds account for €1,277 billion (50%), while foreign investment funds represent €301 billion (12%), and mandates represent €953 billion (38%).

Regarding SFDR classification, €2,443 billion of AUM is categorized as Article 8, and €88 billion as Article 9. Overall, 59% of the assets managed in France, including mandates and domestic and foreign funds, are classified under Article 8 or Article 9, reflecting a strong commitment to sustainable finance among French asset managers.

The AFG[1] report also provides insights into classifications under the AMF (Autorité des Marchés Financiers). In 2023, assets classified under AMF categories 1 and 2 totaled €1,099 billion. Category 1, which includes funds with a significant level of engagement in ESG integration, accounted for €803 billion, while Category 2, involving less engaged ESG approaches, represented €296 billion.

Among Category 1 funds, positive selection strategies such as Best-in-Class, *Best-in-Universe*, and *Best-Effort* dominated the market, comprising 76% of the AUM. For Category 2 funds, 72% of the assets

[1] Source : AFG - file:///C:/Users/hostrowski/Desktop/afg-investissresponsable-web.pdf

incorporate ESG factors directly into the financial analysis and portfolio construction processes, demonstrating an increased sophistication and depth in ESG integration.

While Section 1 presented the regulatory foundations of sustainable finance, including the EU Taxonomy and the SFDR, the real challenge lies in translating these obligations into effective corporate and investment practices. Section 2 shifts the focus from compliance to the practical application of ESG principles within companies and by investors, examining how these frameworks shape strategic and operational decisions in the financial sphere.

2.3 The Integration of ESG Criteria into the Financial Sphere: A Challenge for Investors

Extensive academic research has been conducted to delineate the distinctions between traditional financial reporting and non-financial environmental, social, and governance (ESG) reporting. The literature identifies significant conceptual and methodological challenges inherent to ESG disclosures, stemming from their multidimensional character and the absence of universally harmonized standards. Empirical studies further document the operational difficulties faced by firms, including concerns regarding data verifiability, heterogeneity of reporting frameworks, and the necessity to reconcile heterogeneous stakeholder informational demands. A rigorous examination of these issues is crucial for evaluating the effectiveness, reliability, and credibility of non-financial reporting mechanisms. This body of scholarship thus contributes to a nuanced understanding of the structural limitations within ESG reporting. It elucidates the broader implications for corporate governance practices and the decision-making processes of investors.

2.3.1 Exploring the Foundations of ESG Reporting: Financial Reporting vs Extra-Financial Reporting

The evolution of corporate reporting has extended beyond financial metrics to include independent corporate social responsibility (CSR) reports, often referred to by various nomenclatures such as sustainability reports (Ioannou & Serafeim, 2012; Simnett et al., 2009), accountability reports (Ramanna, 2013), and responsibility reports. These reports underscore the importance of providing key information, a fundamental concept in corporate reporting that fosters greater transparency and accountability to a broader range of stakeholders, including those beyond traditional financial investors. However, the complex and fragmented nature of environmental, social, and governance (ESG) reporting, with its diverse standards and varying materiality definitions, has created a highly complicated and multidimensional ecosystem (Sulkowski & Jebe, 2022).

The ecosystem of ESG reporting encompasses a diverse range of stakeholders, including civil society entities, information intermediaries, and investors. Civil society entities have traditionally promoted the ESG reporting movement, primarily utilizing corporate ESG disclosures. Simultaneously, third-party intermediaries analyze and score companies' ESG performance using corporate reports as their primary data source. In recent years, investors have emerged as significant users of ESG information, incorporating it into their investment choices. The dynamic interplay between these users, reporting businesses, and standard setters determines the trajectory of ESG disclosure standards and practices (Sulkowski & Jebe, 2022).

At the basis of ESG disclosure lies the dual responsibility of reporting firms as producers and users of information. Companies often rely on criteria created by private organizations to generate ESG reports, which stakeholders subsequently use to measure performance or intermediaries to develop ESG ratings. Unlike financial reporting, which is defined by uniform, mandatory standards enforced by governmental regulators, ESG reporting functions within a polycentric system distinguished by voluntary disclosure frameworks. This lack of standardization results in various conceptions of materiality and divergent perceptions of what constitutes meaningful disclosure (Sulkowski & Jebe, 2022).

The content and presentation of ESG reports further underscore this variation. Research reveals that the language and structural characteristics of these reports considerably determine their relevance and credibility. Narrative disclosure has significantly impacted the definition of ESG report utilization. Reports with higher length, a less optimistic tone, and less "stickiness" tend to be more informative and convincing (Caglio et al., 2020; Dyer et al., 2017; Li, 2008; Muslu et al., 2019). Longer reports are associated with better levels of ESG performance (Nazari et al., 2017), whereas companies with inadequate ESG performance tend to adjust their tone to present an excessively optimistic view (Cho et al., 2010; Holder-Webb et al., 2009).

In contrast, financial reporting structures have typically adhered to rigid, legally binding norms designed to prevent information asymmetry and guarantee accountability. These frameworks provide verifiable and standardized information, enforce performance and position reporting, and link managerial actions to outcomes through litigation, audits, and regulatory inspections (Ramanna, 2013). The fundamental elements of financial reporting, verifiability, conservatism, and standardization, protect investors against excessively optimistic reports and build a strong structure for informed decision-making (Ball et al., 2000).

CSR reporting, however, lacks many of these qualities. Despite efforts to standardize CSR reporting and audits, much discretion exists in the degree and scope of disclosures. Even when audited, CSR reports generally focus on processes and governance structures rather than substantive, outcome-based information, allowing firms to exaggerate their positive aspects and overlook areas of poor performance (Mishra & Modi, 2013; Sethi et al., 2015). This decision exacerbates information asymmetry, reducing the credibility and value of CSR reporting for investors.

As the GRI emphasizes, the primary objective of reporting is to foster stakeholder engagement that leads to meaningful changes in corporate choices and behavior (GRI, 2002). Ultimately, the effectiveness of extra-financial reporting depends on its ability to address information asymmetry gaps and foster meaningful dialogue among stakeholders. The ongoing limitations of standardization, combined with opportunistic managerial behavior and greenwashing risks, necessitate frequent assessment and revision of the ESG reporting system to enhance its relevance and effectiveness.

2.3.2 ESG Reporting: Current Challenge for Companies and Investors

Extra-financial reporting has become a significant challenge due to its complexity. A wide range of frameworks and many methodologies have been developed that require more explanation. The coexistence of multiple standards such as GRI, SASB, TCFD, and CSRD creates a fragmented and sometimes contradictory reporting environment that undermines data comparability and reliability. As a result, some researchers confirmed the ineffectiveness of sustainability and ESG reporting in advancing societal sustainability objectives (Dillard et al., 2019; Milne et al., 2013). Research that exposes greenwashing and a concentration on reputation in ESG disclosures increases concerns regarding this ineffectiveness.

Melloni et al. (2017) conclude that enterprises exhibiting worse social indicators provide less clear reports and less information on their sustainability performance. Their findings suggest that early users of Integrated Reports use volume and syntactical reading ease modification, in addition to thematic content and language manipulation, as strategies for impression management. Such rhetorical strategies blur the line between transparent communication and symbolic legitimacy-seeking behaviors.

Waniak et al. (2018) examined 116 corporate reports from various countries, including Poland, the Czech Republic, Hungary, Slovakia, Lithuania, Estonia, Ukraine, and Latvia, to investigate whether companies modify metrics in CSR reports to hide unfavorable information in extra-financial disclosures. Their research demonstrated that firms modify CSR metrics disclosed in CSR reports; nevertheless, they noted that they could not confirm if these modifications were made to enhance the companies' public image. This uncertainty reinforces the idea that ESG reporting often lacks the verifiability and enforcement mechanisms that characterize traditional financial reporting.

In addition, Well et al. (2021) evaluate whether the reporting techniques of LVMH and Kering were legitimate, meaning they conform to established norms, principles, or standards. The research examined their reporting against the generally known GRI criteria for this situation. The investigation reveals that the two companies comply effectively with the GRI rules in certain situations, but in other cases, they do not. Examining the two reports side by side reveals the strengths and weaknesses of each reporting approach. For example, Kering's thorough inclusion of all supply chain factors suggests that LVMH may not include this and could significantly underreport its impacts. Such selective disclosure, or the omission of negative impacts, points to the prevalence of symbolic management strategies that weaken the credibility of reports. This illustrates components of selective reporting and symbolic management, which are likely to impact the company's credibility from the perspective of stakeholders (Ashforth & Gibbs, 1990). These might also be regarded as planned greenwashing (Okereke, 2007), especially considering that the reports are typically inconsistent, selectively presenting positive benefits rather than negative ones. This inconsistency complicates investment decisions and undermines stakeholder trust.

Other researchers focused on the methodological problems associated with ESG and sustainability reporting. Data credibility difficulties present various operational challenges for companies, including issues related to data collection costs, a lack of data exchange throughout the value chain, and unclear regulations surrounding data processing and management. For multinational firms with complex supply chains, collecting granular and verifiable ESG data across different regions remains a significant challenge. These methodological constraints highlight the technical limitations of different impact assessment accounting approaches for diverse environmental and social issues.

Popovic et al. (2018) stated that there is a lack of information for social evaluation and a lack of relevant quantitative social sustainability indicators. Their article proposes a set of 31 quantitative social sustainability indicators that facilitate the evaluation of the supply chain. In particular, the concerns linked to labor practices, decent employment, and human rights are examined. The indicators are developed based on literature research and verified through an in-depth analysis of 141 sustainability reports, covering all levels of the supply chain. Finally, the applicability of the indicators is assessed using data accessible in sustainability reports. Results from the content analysis indicated that companies in their sustainability reports implicitly address all 31 indicators. Furthermore, it was demonstrated how these indicators could be utilized to assess the entire supply chain. Thus, the proposed indicators can be used for both performance assessment and ongoing evaluation of supply chains, serving as a crucial tool in decision-making. However, the lack of harmonized adoption of such indicators across reporting companies limits their scalability and usefulness to investors.

While ESG and sustainability reporting are essential for SMEs, many research studies have highlighted the challenges that SMEs face in relation to ESG reporting. In reality, sustainability reporting for SME supply chains employs standardized reporting frameworks, such as the Global Reporting Initiative (GRI) or the Sustainability Accounting Standards Board (SASB). According to Permatasari and Kosasih (2021), following the GRI can be problematic for SMEs for several reasons: resource restrictions, limited experience, complexity, and time constraints. In addition, Mousa and Ozili (2022) highlighted the infrastructural concerns that must be addressed. Siew et al. (2013) claim that it has to identify metrics and methodologies that would help estimate how sustainable or not existing activities are to construct its infrastructure, which is difficult for SMEs to execute because of the accumulation of additional obstacles, such as a lack of resources, costly expenses, and restricted time. Moreover, ESG data collection and reporting for SMEs are often disproportionate to their financial capacity, leading to low compliance or overly simplified disclosures that lack credibility.

Stakeholders demand a sustainability report because they expect the company to perform responsibly and transparently. Thus, companies face difficulties due to the diverse behaviors of their stakeholders. Each stakeholder has particular informational requirements from the sustainability report (Băndoi et al., 2021). This multiplicity of expectations makes it challenging to produce a report that satisfies investors, regulators, and customers simultaneously. SMEs cannot survive in the global market, which incorporates this sustainability report, due to their lack of knowledge (Xin et al., 2023).

Jiménez et al. (2021) highlighted the complexity of existing sustainability reporting frameworks, which present another significant barrier for SMEs. They also illustrated that the complexity of existing sustainability reporting frameworks is another important obstacle for SMEs. According to them, tools designed to measure sustainability are generally built for large companies and require expertise that SMEs may lack. Sohns et al. (2023) confirmed that adopting sustainability measurements for SMEs requires a significant time investment that would compromise ordinary company operations. The time and resources that SMEs must allocate to create ESG reports, in particular, have a substantial impact on their day-to-day business operations. As a result, many SMEs view ESG reporting as a compliance burden rather than a strategic opportunity, which further delays its adoption.

Lastly, Dissanayake (2021) confirmed that the significant number of key performance indicators in the sustainable report raises another difficulty for SMEs related to updating these indicators. This KPI (Key Performance Indicator) inflation not only overwhelms small businesses but also dilutes the focus of ESG reporting, making it harder for stakeholders to assess what really matters.

2.4 Conclusion

The rise of ESG reporting marks a pivotal shift in corporate disclosure practices, reflecting a growing demand for transparency beyond traditional financial metrics. While the foundations of ESG reporting were built on the ambition to inform stakeholders and foster accountability, the lack of standardization and regulatory enforcement has led to a fragmented and sometimes inconsistent reporting landscape. This polycentric ecosystem, shaped by multiple frameworks, actors, and definitions of materiality, raises questions about the comparability, credibility, and utility of disclosed information.

These structural limitations are compounded by practical challenges faced by both companies and investors. On the one hand, firms must navigate complex and evolving expectations from regulators, civil society, and investors while dealing with methodological issues, high reporting costs, and the risk of greenwashing. On the other hand, investors often struggle to interpret ESG data due to inconsistent metrics, selective disclosures, and a lack of verifiability. For small and medium-sized enterprises (SMEs), these obstacles are amplified by resource constraints and limited internal expertise, making ESG integration even more difficult.

Ultimately, for ESG reporting to fulfill its transformative potential, it must move beyond symbolic compliance and impression management. This requires greater harmonization of standards, more explicit guidance on materiality, and robust assurance mechanisms to reduce information asymmetries and rebuild stakeholder trust. Without these reforms, ESG reporting risks becoming a procedural exercise with limited impact on sustainable corporate behavior and long-term value creation.

References

Ashforth, B. E., & Gibbs, B. W. (1990). The double-edged nature of organizational legitimation. *Organization Science, 1*(2), 177–194.

Ball, R., Kothari, S. P., & Robin, A. (2000). The effect of international institutional factors on properties of accounting earnings. *Journal of Accounting and Economics, 29*(1), 1–51.

Băndoi, A., Bocean, C. G., Del Baldo, M., Mandache, L., Mănescu, L. G., & Sitnikov, C. S. (2021). Including sustainable reporting practices in corporate management reports: Assessing the impact of transparency on economic performance. *Sustainability, 13*(2), 940.

Caglio, A., Melloni, G., & Perego, P. (2020). Informational content and assurance of textual disclosures: Evidence on integrated reporting. *European Accounting Review, 29*(1), 55–83.

Cho, C. H., Roberts, R., & Patten, D. M. (2010). The language of U.S. corporate environmental disclosure. *Accounting, Organizations and Society, 35*(4), 431–443.

Dillard, J., & Vinnari, E. (2019). Critical dialogical accountability: From accounting-based accountability to accountability-based accounting. *Critical Perspectives on Accounting, 62*, 16–38.

Dissanayake, D. (2021). Sustainability key performance indicators and the Global Reporting Initiative: Usage and challenges in a developing country context. *Meditari Accountancy Research, 29*(3), 543–567.

Dyer, T., Lang, M., & Stice-Lawrence, L. (2017). The evolution of 10-K textual disclosure: Evidence from latent Dirichlet allocation. *Journal of Accounting and Economics, 64*(2–3), 221–245.

Global Reporting Initiative. (2002). *Sustainability reporting guidelines*. Retrieved from https://jussemper.org/Newsletters/Resources/gri_2002_guidelines.pdf

Holder-Webb, L., Cohen, J. R., Nath, L., & Wood, D. (2009). The supply of corporate social responsibility disclosures among U.S. firms. *Journal of Business Ethics, 84*(4), 497–527.

Ioannou, I., & Serafeim, G. (2012). What drives corporate social performance? The role of nation-level institutions. *Journal of International Business Studies, 43*(9), 834–864.

Jiménez, E., de la Cuesta-González, M., & Boronat-Navarro, M. (2021). How small and medium-sized enterprises can uptake the sustainable development goals through a cluster management organization: A case study. *Sustainability, 13*(11), 5939.

Li, F. (2008). Annual report readability, current earnings, and earnings persistence. *Journal of Accounting and Economics, 45*(2–3), 221–247.

Melloni, G., Caglio, A., & Perego, P. (2017). Saying more with less? Disclosure conciseness, completeness, and balance in integrated reports. *Journal of Accounting and Public Policy, 36*(3), 220–238.

Milne, M. J., & Gray, R. (2013). W(h)ither ecology? The triple bottom line, the Global Reporting Initiative, and corporate sustainability reporting. *Journal of Business Ethics, 118*, 13–29.

Mishra, D. R., & Modi, S. B. (2013). Positive and negative corporate social responsibility, financial leverage, and idiosyncratic risk. *Journal of Business Ethics, 117*, 431–448.

Mousa, R., & Ozili, P. K. (2022). A futuristic view of using XBRL technology in non-financial sustainability reporting: The case of the FDIC. *Journal of Risk and Financial Management, 16*(1), 1.

Muslu, V., Mutlu, S., Radhakrishnan, S., & Tsang, A. (2019). Corporate social responsibility report narratives and analyst forecast accuracy. *Journal of Business Ethics, 154*(4), 1119–1142.

Nazari, J. A., Hrazdil, K., & Mahmoudian, F. (2017). Assessing social and environmental performance through narrative complexity in CSR reports. *Journal of Contemporary Accounting & Economics, 13*(2), 166–178.

Okereke, C. (2007). An exploration of motivations, drivers, and barriers to carbon management: The UK FTSE 100. *European Management Journal, 25*(6), 475–486.

Permatasari, P., & Kosasih, E. (2021). Sustainability reporting guideline for small and medium enterprises (SMEs): Case study from 25 SMEs in Indonesia. *RSF Conference Series: Business, Management and Social Sciences, 1*(2), 10–20.

Popovic, T., et al. (2018). Quantitative indicators for social sustainability assessment of supply chains. *Journal of Cleaner Production, 180*, 748–768.

Ramanna, K. (2013). A framework for research on corporate accountability reporting. *Accounting Horizons, 27*(2), 409–432.

Sethi, S. P., Martell, T. F., & Demir, M. (2015). An evaluation of the quality of corporate social responsibility reports by some of the world's largest financial institutions. Journal of Business Ethics, 1–19.

Siew, R. Y. J., Balatbat, M. C. A., & Carmichael, D. G. (2013). A review of building/infrastructure sustainability reporting tools (SRTs). *Smart and Sustainable Built Environment, 2*(2), 106–139.

Simnett, R., Vanstraelen, A., & Chua, W. (2009). Assurance on sustainability reports: An international comparison. *The Accounting Review, 84*(3), 937–967.

Sohns, T. M., Aysolmaz, B., Figge, L., & Joshi, A. (2023). Green business process management for business sustainability: A case study of manufacturing small and medium-sized enterprises (SMEs) from Germany. *Journal of Cleaner Production, 401*, 136667.

Sulkowski, A., & Jebe, R. (2022). Evolving ESG reporting governance, regime theory, and proactive law: Predictions and strategies. *American Business Law Journal, 59*(3), 449–503. https://doi.org/10.1111/ablj.12210

Waniak-Michalak, H., Sapkauskiene, A., & Leitonienė, S. (2018). Do companies manipulate CSR information to retain legitimacy? *Engineering Economics, 29*(3), 352–360.

Wells, V., Athwal, N., Nervino, E., & Carrigan, M. (2021). How legitimate are the environmental sustainability claims of luxury conglomerates? *Journal of Fashion Marketing and Management: An International Journal, 25*(4), 697–722.

Xin, Y., Khan, R. U., Dagar, V., & Qian, F. (2023). Do international resources configure SMEs' sustainable performance in the digital era? Evidence from Pakistan. *Resources Policy, 80*, 103169.

CHAPTER 3

ESG Performance and Financial Performance: An Overview

Baran Siyahhan and Marie-Renée Loucou

Abstract This chapter synthesizes the main theoretical and empirical developments surrounding the relationship between ESG analysis and corporate performance, both financial and extra-financial. Building on the historical and regulatory foundations outlined in previous chapters, it explores how organizations integrate ESG concerns into their strategic and reporting frameworks in response to growing societal expectations and stakeholder pressures.

The first section provides a theoretical lens for understanding ESG dynamics, drawing from legitimacy, stakeholder, and signaling theories. These frameworks explain how firms engage in ESG reporting to gain social legitimacy, respond to stakeholder demands, and signal responsible behavior in markets characterized by information asymmetries.

The second section reviews empirical evidence on the relationship between ESG performance and financial outcomes. While some studies suggest ESG practices can enhance firm value through reputation, efficiency, and innovation, others find mixed or even negative effects, particularly for

B. Siyahhan (✉) • M.-R. Loucou
ICL, Junia, Université Catholique de Lille, LITL
e-mail: baran.siyahhan@univ-catholille.fr

S. Kendo (ed.), *Non-Financial Reporting and ESG Performance*,
Palgrave Studies in Impact Finance,
https://doi.org/10.1007/978-3-032-19092-5_3

SMEs. Factors such as industry sector, firm size, and the nature of ESG activities influence outcomes. The chapter also details how ESG impacts valuation, including product-market perception, risk reduction, cost of capital, and consumer behavior.

Finally, the chapter highlights critical limitations in ESG research, notably the lack of focus on SMEs and VSEs, whose limited resources and reporting capacities challenge ESG integration.

Keywords ESG Performance • Financial Performance • Stakeholder • Signaling

3.1 Introduction

Despite increasing interest and a growing body of literature over the past decade, the core principles of Corporate Social Responsibility (CSR) and Environmental, Social, and Governance (ESG) factors are not a new concept (Nirino et al., 2021). As early as the 1970s, Meadows et al. (1972, p. 23) warned that continued growth trends in population and economic activity, combined with pollution and limited resources, could eventually lead to a collapse in both population and industrial capacity. Essentially, both CSR and ESG are activities that support companies in achieving sustainability (MacNeil & Esser, 2022).

The concept of Corporate Social Responsibility (CSR) and how companies, both large and small, approach CSR have faced considerable changes over the past few decades (MacNeil & Esser, 2022). The landscape has shifted from one where the "social responsibility of the business is to increase its profits" (Friedman, 1970) to a growing recognition that firms are an integral, if not the most crucial, part of the transition modern society must make to face the challenge of climate change.

Over the years, two simultaneous shifts have taken place: first, at a more conceptual level, voluntary CSR activities have evolved into companies' environmental, social, and governance (ESG) profiles, which are surveyed, reported, and increasingly regulated. Numerous institutions, including KLD, Sustainalytics, and Moody's, among others, assess and rank companies based on various ESG criteria (Berg et al., 2022). Investors look increasingly to companies' ESG profiles when making investment decisions and assessing risk. Second, and linked to the conceptual shift, the discourse on company behavior has shifted away from voluntary actions to mandatory disclosures, tighter regulation, and growing stakeholder activism (Bardos et al., 2020; dos Reis Cardillo & Cruz Basso, 2025). The latter reflects another crucial conceptual shift: the idea that companies are accountable not only to their shareholders but to stakeholders[1] has gained traction.

These changes require many companies to adopt a green business model, achieve social and community goals, and report on their progress in these areas. Each of these activities may involve significant costs, especially for SMEs. Therefore, a legitimate question is whether it pays to undertake the necessary investments and become greener. What is the impact of such investments on companies' financial performance? Reinhardt (1999) suggests that these questions should be addressed as other business problems, and managers should question under what circumstances environmental investments would benefit shareholders. However, given the shift in the landscape, meeting ESG performance criteria becomes less of an option. Therefore, this chapter explores the relation between corporate ESG performance and financial performance. Before investigating this relation, the chapter reviews the evolution of the theoretical framework and the major theories that shape the literature on companies' approach to CSR/ESG.

3.2 Theoretical Framework

In the aftermath of the Global Financial Crisis (GFC) of 2008–2009 and the controversy surrounding the financial sector that preceded and occurred during the crisis[2], organizations have focused their efforts on environmental, social, and governance (ESG) performance. The governance scandals that came to light following the GFC have led to widespread public outcry concerning incentives and financial regulation and focused attention on how companies interact with various stakeholders (MacNeil & Esser, 2022). Thus, using the means of pressure such as regulation, opinion campaigns, calls for boycotts and litigation, social community (public authorities, civil society, non-governmental organizations (NGOs)), operational partners (customers, suppliers, banks, insurance companies), internal stakeholders (employees, trade unions and shareholders) are now partners

[1] Freeman (1984) defines stakeholders as "any group or individual who can affect or who can be affected by the achievement of organizational objectives." Other authors such as Mercier (1999) and Donaldson and Preston (1995) have also proposed definitions.

[2] See Eberle et al. (2013); Chae and Park (2018).

of companies affecting and participating in the decision-making process (Lépineux, 2003). This situation has essentially resulted in the substantial disclosure of ESG performance, notably through the publication of non-financial reports in response to moral and regulatory pressures (Li et al., 2018).

Societal concerns today place companies (large, medium, and small alike) at the center stage of corporate and environmental sustainability (Crutzen & Van Caillie, 2010; Delchet, 2004). Company performance is no longer measured exclusively in financial terms but incorporates social and environmental factors to comprise a three-dimensional measure. The post-crisis context has necessitated that ESG criteria be considered to ensure transparency for stakeholders. This has led to the establishment of an international normative framework, such as the GRI standards, to measure companies' progress in sustainable development. Furthermore, companies are more willing to communicate their level of progress (through labeling, social reports, social audits, etc.) to stakeholders. Global economic turbulence has severely hampered these efforts, but some countries, such as France, have maintained their green policy through the national French Tech "Green 20" program.

Various scientific studies have explored the implications of ESG performance and sustainability (i.e., ESG) reporting between organizations and stakeholders, aiming to understand the underlying theories. Three main economic theories can be used to capture the inclusion of ESG aspects into a company's overall performance. These are neo-institutional or legitimacy theory, stakeholder theory, and signal theory, all of which contribute to a clearer vision of the phenomenon.

3.2.1 Neo-Institutional (Legitimacy) Theory

Neo-institutional or legitimacy theory sets out the theoretical framework for responding to institutional pressures[3] through ESG efforts. Inspired by the work of Selznick (1949), this approach emphasizes organizational constraints during the company's evolution (Meyer et al., 1991). This theory compares the commitment and values of managers with the social environment to which they belong. The non-financial reporting stimulated by this confrontation will enable the evaluation of the effectiveness of regulations, beliefs, and standards. A company is thus bound to its social or cultural environment by a social contract and voluntarily communicates

[3] Mimetic (competitive pressures), normative and coercive (laws and regulations).

its ESG performance. It benefits from the legitimacy[4] it needs to prosper, provided it meets socially responsible requirements (Hatch, 2000). The institutional vision considers a company to be legitimate when its means and ends appear to be in line with society's values, social norms, and expectations (Ashforth & Gibbs, 1990; Scott, 2001). However, companies may incur costs associated with pursuing legitimacy. The adoption of socially responsible practices can, unfortunately, be perceived as suspicious due to a quest for financial performance.

3.2.1.1 Principle of Legitimacy

Legitimacy in the Habermas (1978) sense extends beyond laws emanating from empowered institutions and encompasses consciousness and values. The notion of legitimacy refers to a symbol of collective evaluation, and therefore to external validation (Stone & Brush, 1996). It necessarily involves a social judgment of the stakeholders only and solely from this point of view (Zimmerman & Zeitz, 2002; Ashforth & Gibbs, 1990). As a result, the legitimacy sought by companies can come from a variety of sources and can also take many different forms. These include traditional legitimacy based on customs and tradition, charismatic legitimacy based on the leader's exceptional character, and rational legitimacy based on impersonal, rational laws and rules (Weber, 1971). In terms of its forms, legitimacy is achieved through the consent of the many players in the company's social environment. This status is more about an ongoing and consistently problematic process, as social values and expectations continually change. Moreover, the orientation of legitimacy criteria is often contradictory. Achieving a legitimate status is now seen not only as a business strategy but also as a resource for enhancing the company's attractiveness. Let us not forget that the company has its traditional objectives of growth and survival in mind. In this case, it needs investors who use legitimacy as a positive signal, as well as other stakeholders.

3.2.1.2 Legitimacy Dimensions

The various aspects of legitimacy stem from institutional pressures in the company's environment. According to Scott (1995), a distinction is made between normative legitimacy, regulatory legitimacy, and cognitive

[4] Suchman (1995) defines legitimacy as: "a generalized perception or presumption that an entity's actions are desirable, proper, or appropriate within a socially constructed system of norms, values, beliefs, and definitions."

legitimacy. Several controls and regulatory structures ensure order and stability in the environment. It is no longer just a question of strategic commercial behavior, but of explicit legal constraints that justify legitimacy and, conversely, are liable to (coercive) sanction. Normative legitimacy is based on both social values and norms to the extent that legitimacy can be granted by other organizations, constituting a vote of confidence (Zimmerman & Zeitz, 2002, p. 419).

Originating in the field of social psychology (Berger & Luckmann, 2016), cognitive legitimacy refers to rules that provide plausible explanations for the behavior of institutions (Ruef & Scott, 1998, p. 879). Lamertz and Baum (1998) highlight how individuals should behave according to cognitive rules and categorizations. Other authors (Suchman, 1995; Scott, 1995) have proposed a categorization of legitimacy, emphasizing elements of calculation and self-interest.

According to the neo-institutional theory, institutional pressures stemming from all three legitimacy dimensions influence corporate CSR policies and ESG engagement (Gao-Zeller et al., 2019). Apart from regulatory pressures, corporations are often compelled to follow the example of other similar companies in an effort to reduce uncertainty (Golrida et al., 2020). Furthermore, Baughn et al. (2007) present evidence of cross-country variation in corporations' CSR engagement. For instance, companies in Japan, Taiwan, and Singapore tend to be more active in CSR policies than companies in Pakistan or Bangladesh. This indicates the importance of social and economic context in the adoption of CSR policies. However, it is also important to bear in mind that engagement in CSR activities can also be an avenue for differentiation and gaining stakeholder trust in weak regulatory and institutional settings (Li et al., 2025).

3.2.2 *Stakeholder Theory*

Often juxtaposed with the shareholder value maximization theory, stakeholder theory plays a crucial role in considering ESG performance and its impact on stakeholders. Corporate social responsibility requires companies to consider the interests of all stakeholders affected by their actions. This theory sheds light on the power of stakeholders and explains how their relationship influences corporate commitment. This relationship can be measured through non-financial reporting, a guarantee of transparency, and the extent to which the demands, recommendations, and suggestions of stakeholders are considered. Minutolo et al. (2019) argue that increased transparency enhances business value and operational efficiency.

The origins of stakeholder theory can be traced back to the work of Dodd (1931) and Barnard (1938). The latter focused on issues of cooperation and goal achievement. They consider divergent interests to be an obstacle to achieving mutually beneficial partnerships and, consequently, practical cooperation. This theory differs from that of the organization[5] in its normative character and the equivalence of interests. Corporate profit is no longer conceived from a single angle, notably that of shareholders, but rather integrates a pluralist approach that considers all stakeholders. Martinet and Reynaud (2015) rightly point out that American firms have shifted from a shareholder approach to a stakeholder approach. Companies divide their efforts between the stakeholders and optimize information to avoid any confrontation with stakeholders (Damak-Ayadi, 2003). In this respect, establishing and maintaining relationships with various stakeholders is crucial for enhancing company performance.

The stakeholder theory makes two key assumptions and entails three different approaches. The two main assumptions are:

- Hypothesis 1. Every company affects and is affected by its relations with any individual or group of individuals in the achievement of its objectives.
- Hypothesis 2. Any interest defended by the stakeholders is equivalent and has the same intrinsic value.

Stakeholders' theory, in line with the work of Donaldson and Preston (1995), is based on three main approaches: descriptive, instrumental and normative. The two first approaches are part of empirical theory. Although these theories may reject the normative approach (parallelism), they seem to grow out of each other (symbiosis). They even appear to complement each other and form part of the same theoretical framework (integration).

The descriptive approach focuses on describing the characteristics and behaviors of managers and different stakeholders. It focuses on the management of firms according to their typology (Brenner & Cochran, 1991; Kaler, 2003), the way organizations are thought of and managed (Brenner

[5] John R. Commons' "going concern" analysis considers individuals under the domination of the same operating rules and emphasizes the transition from purely individual futures to a collective, shared future (Gislain, 2002).

& Molander, 1977; Clarkson, 1991), the importance of stakeholders and the dissemination of societal information (Moneva & Llena, 2000; Jawahar & Mclaughlin, 2001; Freeman et al., 2004; Agoraki et al., 2023).

The instrumental approach focuses on the relationship between stakeholder management policy and achieving profitability objectives. Initiated by Jones (1995), the instrumental approach to stakeholder theory considers that, all other things being equal, companies with a stakeholder management policy will perform better.

The normative approach sets out the fundamental principles of stakeholder theory, emphasizing the manager's moral obligations towards all stakeholders. It also considers that all the interests defended by stakeholders are equivalent and not a means to the ends of other stakeholders (Evan & Freeman, 1988). It is therefore up to the company to balance and address various interests while ensuring that it prioritizes at least those of its shareholders. Coordinating stakeholders' interests presupposes that no single dimension of overall performance predominates (Hahn et al., 2018).

The normative approach has often been integrated with the "resource-based view of the firm" (RBV), which considers scarce, valuable, and inimitable resources as a means of achieving high performance, creating competitive advantages, and significantly impacting the company's sustainability (Barney, 1991). Freeman et al. (2021) advocate for merging these theories due to the sustainable competitive advantages generated by strategic capital, as evoked by RBV theory. Sustainability is only effective when there are links between stakeholders, which also influence ESG practices. It is easy to see why the above-mentioned merger should be seen in the light of companies' ESG commitments.

3.2.3 Signaling Theory

Signaling theory is one of the cornerstones of the economics of information (Stiglitz, 2000). The economics of information deals with settings where parties, whether individuals or institutions, have varying degrees of information that they can act on, depending on their incentives. Information asymmetry naturally arises in principal-agent frameworks (e.g., managers versus creditors of a company), financial markets (e.g., large investors versus small investors), competitive settings (e.g., two rival companies in a duopoly), and labor markets (e.g., job seekers versus employers). In settings where parties have unobservable attributes such as competence or product quality, a credible signal can help differentiate one party from others (Spence, 1973; King et al., 2005). For instance, a degree from a well-renowned college can signal a job candidate's competence, and a quality certification can indicate the quality of a product.

dos Reis Cardillo and Cruz Basso (2025) argue that corporate CSR/ESG activities can signal a company's commitment to ethical behavior and build a reputation that, in turn, can attract investors and consumers. Importantly, Su et al. (2016) point out that a commitment to CSR/ESG policies constitutes a credible signal, as it is costly and the premium from these activities often compensates only for their costs in high-quality corporations. In other words, CSR engagement enables companies to differentiate themselves from competitors by sending stakeholders companies' unobservable attributes (King et al., 2005).

There is some evidence that CSR/ESG engagement signals product quality (Bardos et al., 2020). Affolter et al. (2024) find that sustainability-linked bonds (SLBs) send a credible signal to the market when they are linked to renewable energy or energy efficiency, but induce no market reaction when they aim to reduce greenhouse gas emissions.

3.3 Financial and Non-financial Performance: An Exploration of Empirical Results and Discussion

Adoption of socially responsible policies by companies today appears to be a strategic behavior and a means of gaining a competitive advantage through ethics, sustainability, adherence, and reputation (Forcadell & Aracil, 2017; Konar & Cohen, 2001). The valuation of companies has thus evolved; it now increasingly takes into account the societal functions of the company. These are no longer solely economic and financial, but also social and environmental. ESG impact is becoming one of the main determinants of investor decision-making (Kiymaz, 2012).

Two opposing visions exist: one presenting extra-financial performance as an obstacle to financial performance and growth, and the other (social) as an investment with a positive impact on the company's legitimacy, reputation, and profitability. Thus, the integration of ESG objectives now appears as a strategic behavior linked to the performance attribute generated by environmental standards and values (Porter et al., 2019). Companies' responses to societal, environmental, and social demands are reflected in the repositioning of their product offerings. Beyond obligations and willingness, the adoption of these one-off or gradual practices will depend on the sector of activity and the ability to implement a sustainable plan (Lubin & Esty, 2010).

The connection between corporate social performance (CSP) and corporate financial performance (CFP) has been the subject of numerous empirical studies over the past decade. Despite some studies finding a negative or insignificant relationship, there is substantial evidence indicating a positive relationship between ESG and CFP.

At first glance, CSR/ESG activities may be perceived as a deviation from a company's main goal of profit maximization and shareholder value creation. As such, Friedman (2007) argues that the costs associated with ESG activities would have a negative impact on companies' financial performance. Disclosure of ESG performance imposes costs that outweigh the benefits and lead to misallocation of corporate resources. Several authors reveal a negative or zero relationship between financial and extra-financial performance (Clacher & Hagendorff, 2012; Di Giuli & Kostovetsky, 2014; Kruger, 2015). Furthermore, Margolis and Walsh (2003) reported mixed results. For example, some studies (Brooks & Oikonomou, 2018; Friede et al., 2015) show a moderately positive relationship, while others report neither a significant nor a neutral relationship (Aupperle et al., 1985; McWilliams & Siegel, 2000). However, it appears that these higher costs associated with implementing ESG initiatives and increased disclosure of ESG performance may be easier for larger companies to achieve.

According to stakeholder and legitimacy theory, when a company enhances its ESG performance to meet stakeholder expectations, it gains greater support, better opportunities, and lower transaction costs (Fombrun et al., 2000; Arian et al., 2023). This improvement in financial performance benefits all stakeholders and the broader economy (Limkriangkrai et al., 2017; Nazari et al., 2017). As a result, companies will focus on developing their human capital, innovating, and refining processes to better serve their customers. Hopner and Yu (2010) found a positive link between corporate social performance and financial performance in specific industries, especially consumer discretionary and healthcare. The authors' findings in the consumer sector are supported, while those in the industrial sector are contradicted according to Baron et al. (2011). Additionally, Lee and Isa (2023) report a positive correlation between ESG practices and corporate financial performance, indicating that adopting ESG can increase corporate value. Habib and Mourad (2024), based on a study of 406 US companies that implemented ESG practices during the COVID-19 pandemic, conclude that ESG reporting has a positive influence on company performance.

Several studies investigate the effect of CSP on CFP from a risk perspective or in various corporate settings, such as mergers and acquisitions (M&As). Giese et al. (2019) establish a causal link between ESG rating improvement and company valuation. The article shows that companies that improve their ESG ranking experience a significant decline in systematic risk (i.e., their beta) and negative idiosyncratic events. Serafeim (2020) identifies a significant relationship between ESG performance and ESG momentum (either positive or negative). It concludes that this interaction has an impact on company value and generates positive alpha. In the context of M&A, Deng et al. (2013) reveal that the ESG/CSR ranking of acquiring companies has a positive impact on post-M&A announcement returns and operating income. In addition, M&A transactions initiated by acquirers with higher ESG rankings are completed more quickly and are less likely to result in job losses.

Environmental performance can be positively related to asset returns (King & Lenox, 2002), which aligns with some meta-analysis studies (Endrikat et al., 2014). According to the resource-based view theory, companies that publish more information about their ESG performance have the motivation and resources to derive financial benefits from this information and achieve a higher market value in the equity market (Hart, 1995; Russo & Fouts, 1997). Dumitrescu and Zakriya (2021) suggest that companies' social performance can mitigate future stock price crashes. They stress; nevertheless, that social factors such as strong employee relations and community initiatives are the main drivers in mitigating the crash risk.

Consumers are an important channel that can explain the link between companies' CSR/ESG activities and value creation. Indeed, Baskentli et al. (2019) find that consumers who are aware of ESG issues also seek out companies that are aware of the same issues. Consequently, companies' ESG/CSR performance and activities create a relationship of trust (Kim & Park, 2020; Castro-Gonzalez et al., 2021), and consumers are more willing to buy and pay a premium for products from these companies (Castro-Gonzalez et al., 2021; Wei et al., 2018). Additionally, professional customers can play a crucial role in ESG/CSR activities within their value chain (Dai et al., 2021). Companies' innovation capacity is yet another channel through which ESG factors potentially affect corporate financial performance. Broadstock et al. (2020) explore the effect of Japanese companies' commitment to ESG activities on their innovation capacity. Although they find a positive impact, they highlight that the effect is nonlinear and industry-specific.

Researchers have examined the link between the financing channel and a company's ESG/CSR profile. This raises two questions: firstly, what impact do ESG profile and performance have on a company's cost of capital and indebtedness? Secondly, do banks consider a company's ESG/CSR profile when tailoring loans? By reducing the costs of capital, improving performance, and enhancing their ESG profile, companies can lead to higher valuations. El Ghoul et al. (2011) find a negative association between companies' CSR/ESG rankings and the cost of equity capital. Kling et al. (2021) studied climate risk exposure and its impact on the cost of capital. Their study accounts for the higher cost of capital in countries more exposed to climate risk. It also shows that companies in these countries maintain a lower debt ratio than those in less exposed countries. In a study examining the relationship between environmental risk and capital structure, Chang et al. (2021) found that climate risk is associated with a decrease in debt levels. Moreover, this decrease is more pronounced for companies covered by analysts and therefore have high visibility.

Climate risk can also affect the terms and conditions of loans granted by banks and the rates of bonds issued by companies. These conditions are the subject of numerous studies. Climate risk is associated with higher spreads (Allman, 2022; Javadi & Masum, 2021; Bos et al., 2022; Ehlers et al., 2022; Fard et al., 2020). Allman (2022) and Ehlers et al. (2022) report that this increase is even more pronounced after the 2015 Paris Agreement. Moreover, regarding bank lending conditions, the findings indicate a negative relationship between loan maturity and risk exposure level, as well as fewer banks participating in the syndicate (Javadi & Masum, 2021; Fard et al., 2020). Conclusions on loan covenants are more mixed: Javadi and Masum (2021) report a higher number of loan covenants, while Fard et al. (2020) conclude that there is no significant impact on loan covenants. Overall, the studies suggest that banks do take climate risk into account in their lending decisions, and consequently, the cost of debt tends to rise, pushing up companies' cost of capital.

3.4 Conclusion

Most studies on the relation between CSP and CFP tend to focus on large companies and multinational companies (MNCs). However, to the extent that large companies begin to implement environmental and social actions, SMEs in the value chain become increasingly concerned about these actions. Furthermore, the European Corporate Sustainability Reporting Directive (CSRD) requires companies above a specific size to report any risks and opportunities that arise from their environmental and social issues[6]. The CSRD envisages a progressive application of disclosure requirements, including SMEs

Micro, small, and medium-sized enterprises (MSMEs) comprise a substantial portion of the global economy: 90% of businesses worldwide are MSMEs, accounting for 60–70% of employment and 50% of GDP (ElTarabishy & Baldegger, 2024). As such, MSMEs are at the forefront of the transition to a more sustainable economic model. However, MSMEs often lack the financial and human resources that big corporations have at their disposal to implement ecological and social transition. Taking this into account, the EU Commission decided to simplify and reduce the complexity of requirements for SMEs. Therefore, it is important to investigate the relation between CSP and CFP for MSMEs.

While big companies have attracted more attention, several studies have explored the relationship between CSP and CFP for SMEs. Gholami et al. (2022) reveal that improving ESG performance is beneficial in the long term for all large-company stakeholders, except for SMEs. They were preceded by Minutolo et al. (2019), who found a negative impact on Tobin's Q and ROA for small companies, while having a significant impact on large companies. Gjergji et al. (2021) find that, unlike large companies, SMEs experience an increase in their cost of capital in response to environmental disclosure. Interestingly, the negative impact of environmental disclosure on the cost of capital is reversed for family-owned SMEs. This suggests that ownership structure can be a moderating factor in the relation between CSP and CFP.

Other papers have also investigated SME characteristics such as resources and size. Cormier and Magnan (1999) highlight the trade-offs that exist between ESG performance disclosure and company characteristics. They are joined by other authors (Yoon & Chung, 2018; Drempetic et al., 2020) who define these characteristics in terms of size, reputation, management structure, and so on.

One particular challenge in the literature is that since most studies are tailored to large companies, ESG scores could be distorted in the case of SMEs. However, during the COVID-19 pandemic, Kusumaningtias

[6] European Commission.

et al. (2021) showed how the elements of responsiveness, responsibility, adequacy, and effectiveness can encourage horizontal and vertical accountability in SMEs. Moreover, the integration of CSR into SMEs' management control systems has been found to play an important role in the relationship between CSR initiatives and organizational performance (Cheffi et al., 2021). The effect of CSP and the changing regulatory landscape on SME financial performance will be an interesting area of research.

In addition, several methodological challenges plague the literature. One important issue is the abundance and divergence of ESG ratings. That is, a company may have widely differing ratings from different institutions based on the same ESG disclosure. Several papers have addressed this phenomenon and examined its implications (See Berg et al., 2022; Chatterji et al., 2016; Christensen et al., 2022; Dumrose et al., 2022; Brandon et al., 2021). ESG ratings divergence can have significant implications since investors and managers rely on these ratings to evaluate performance and take action accordingly (Berg et al., 2022; Chatterji et al., 2016). Brandon et al. (2021) indeed find a positive relation between stock returns and higher ESG rating disagreement. This result suggests an additional premium on equity capital, leading to a higher cost of capital. Christensen et al. (2022) document that increased ESG disclosure can lead to greater disagreement in ESG ratings. They also find that greater ESG ratings divergence is linked to greater return volatility and reduces the likelihood of access to external financing.

Why do ESG ratings diverge? Berg et al. (2022) identify three sources of divergence: (i) different institutions may define different criteria to evaluate a company's ESG performance (scope divergence); (ii) even when rating institutions agree on the criteria, they may use different indicators to proxy for the criteria (measurement divergence); and (iii) the weights used in evaluating ESG criteria can vary across institutions (weight divergence). Berg et al. (2022) decompose ESG ratings divergence into these three components and show that measurement divergence is the most significant source of ESG ratings divergence. Overall, measurement divergence accounts for 56% of the divergence.

Despite the challenges, the literature on the relation between CSP and CFP is likely to grow in the future. The debate appears to have shifted from whether CSR/ESG action is beneficial to corporations to the channels through which these actions impact corporate performance. It is also likely that researchers will increasingly explore how MSMEs are affected both by other companies' CSR/ESG policies and the changing regulatory landscape.

References

Affolter, B., Ciarla, E., Meyer, J., & Sugandhita, S. (2024). Signaling sustainability: Differential reaction of the stock market following the announcement of sustainability-linked bonds. *Finance Research Letters, 63*, 105261.

Agoraki, M. E. K., Giaka, M., Konstantios, D., & Patsika, V. (2023). Firms' sustainability, financial performance, and regulatory dynamics: Evidence from European firms. *Journal of International Money and Finance.*

Allman, E. (2022). Pricing climate change risk in corporate bonds. *Journal of Asset Management, 23*(7), 596–618.

Arian, A., Sands, J., & Tooley, S. (2023). Industry and stakeholder impacts on corporate social responsibility (CSR) and financial performance: Consumer vs. industrial sectors. *Sustainability, 15*(16), 12254.

Ashforth, B. E., & Gibbs, B. W. (1990). The double-edged nature of organizational legitimation. *Organization Science, 1*(2), 177–194.

Aupperle, K. E., Carroll, A. B., & Hatfield, J. D. (1985). An empirical examination of the relationship between corporate social responsibility and profitability. *Academy of Management Journal, 28*(2), 446–463.

Bardos, K. S., Ertugrul, M., & Gao, L. S. (2020). Corporate social responsibility, product market perception, and firm value. *Journal of Corporate Finance, 62*, 101588.

Barnard, C. I. (1938/1974). The executive functions. In J. M. Shafritz, & J. S. Ott (Eds.), *Classic readings in organizational behavior* (pp. 181–188). Wadsworth.

Barney, J. (1991). Firm resources and sustained competitive advantage. *Journal of Management, 17*(1), 99–120.

Baron, D. P., Harjoto, M. A., & Jo, H. (2011). The economics and politics of corporate social performance. *Business and Politics, 13*(2), 1–46.

Baskentli, S., Sen, S., Du, S., & Bhattacharya, C. B. (2019). Consumer reactions to corporate social responsibility: The role of CSR domains. *Journal of Business Research, 95*, 502–513.

Baughn, C. C., Bodie, N. L., & McIntosh, J. C. (2007). Corporate social and environmental responsibility in Asian countries and other geographical regions. *Corporate Social Responsibility and Environmental Management, 14*(4), 189–205.

Berg, F., Kölbel, J. F., & Rigobon, R. (2022). Aggregate confusion: The divergence of ESG ratings. *Review of Finance, 26*(6), 1315–1344.

Berger, P., & Luckmann, T. (2016). The social construction of reality. In W. Longhofer, & D. Winchester (Eds.), *Social theory re-wired: New connections to classical and contemporary perspectives* (pp. 110–122). Routledge.

Bos, J. W., Li, R., & Sanders, M. W. (2022). Hazardous lending: The impact of natural disasters on bank asset portfolios. *Economic Modelling, 108*, 105760.

Brenner, S. N., & Cochran, P. (1991, July). The stakeholder theory of the firm: Implications for business and society theory and research. In *Proceedings of the International Association for Business and Society* (Vol. 2, pp. 897–933). https://doi.org/10.5840/iabsproc1991235

Brenner, S. N., & Molander, E. A. (1977). Is ethics of business changing? *Harvard Business Review, 55*(1), 57–71.

Broadstock, D. C., Matousek, R., Meyer, M., & Tzeremes, N. G. (2020). Does corporate social responsibility impact firms' innovation capacity? The indirect link between environmental, social and governance implementation and innovation performance. *Journal of Business Research, 119*, 99–110. https://doi.org/10.1016/j.jbusres.2019.07.014

Brooks, C., & Oikonomou, I. (2018). The effects of environmental, social and governance disclosures and performance on firm value: A review of the literature in accounting and finance. *The British Accounting Review, 50*(1), 1–15. https://doi.org/10.1016/j.bar.2017.11.005

Castro-González, S., Bande, B., & Fernández-Ferrín, P. (2021). Influence of companies' credibility and trust in corporate social responsibility aspects of consumer food products: The moderating intervention of consumer integrity. *Sustainable Production and Consumption, 28*, 129–141. https://doi.org/10.1016/j.spc.2021.03.032

Chae, B., & Park, E. (2018). Corporate social responsibility (CSR): A survey of topics and trends using Twitter data and topic modeling. *Sustainability, 10*(7), 2231. https://doi.org/10.3390/su10072231

Chang, X., Fu, K., Li, T., Tam, L., & Wong, G. (2021). *Corporate environmental liabilities and capital structure* (SSRN Working Paper No. 3200991). https://doi.org/10.2139/ssrn.3200991

Chatterji, A. K., Durand, R., Levine, D. I., & Touboul, S. (2016). Do ratings of firms converge? Implications for managers, investors and strategy researchers. *Strategic Management Journal, 37*(8), 1597–1614. https://doi.org/10.1002/smj.2407

Cheffi, W., Abdel-Maksoud, A., & Farooq, M. O. (2021). CSR initiatives, organizational performance and the mediating role of integrating CSR into management control systems: Testing an inclusive model within SMEs in an emerging economy. *Journal of Management Control, 32*(3), 333–367. https://doi.org/10.1007/s00187-021-00316-8

Christensen, D. M., Serafeim, G., & Sikochi, A. (2022). Why is corporate virtue in the eye of the beholder? The case of ESG ratings. *The Accounting Review, 97*(1), 147–175. https://doi.org/10.2308/TAR-2019-0506

Clacher, I., & Hagendorff, J. (2012). Do announcements about corporate social responsibility create or destroy shareholder wealth? Evidence from the UK. *Journal of Business Ethics, 106*(3), 253–266. https://doi.org/10.1007/s10551-011-1004-9

Clarkson, M. B. E. (1991). Defining, evaluating, and managing corporate social performance: The stakeholder management model. *Research in Corporate Social Performance and Policy, 12*, 331–358.

Cormier, D., & Magnan, M. (1999). Corporate environmental disclosure strategies: Determinants, costs and benefits. *Journal of Accounting, Auditing & Finance, 14*(4), 429–451. https://doi.org/10.1177/0148558X9901400403

Crutzen, N., & Van Caillie, D. (2010). Le pilotage et la mesure de la performance globale de l'entreprise. *Humanisme et Entreprise, 297*(2), 13–32.

Dai, R., Liang, H., & Ng, L. (2021). Socially responsible corporate customers. *Journal of Financial Economics, 142*(2), 598–626. https://doi.org/10.1016/j.jfineco.2020.08.003

Damak-Ayadi, S. (2003). La théorie des parties prenantes: Théorie empirique ou théorie normative? *In 24ème congrès de l'Association Francophone de Comptabilité* (pp. 1–20). Association Francophone de Comptabilité.

Delchet, K. (2004). *Qu'est-ce que le développement durable?* AFNOR.

Deng, X., Kang, J. K., & Low, B. S. (2013). Corporate social responsibility and stakeholder value maximization: Evidence from mergers. *Journal of Financial Economics, 110*(1), 87–109. https://doi.org/10.1016/j.jfineco.2013.04.014

Di Giuli, A., & Kostovetsky, L. (2014). Are red or blue companies more likely to go green? Politics and corporate social responsibility. *Journal of Financial Economics, 111*(1), 158–180. https://doi.org/10.1016/j.jfineco.2013.10.002

Dodd, E. M., Jr. (1931). For whom are corporate managers trustees? *Harvard Law Review, 45*, 1145–1163.

Donaldson, T., & Preston, L. E. (1995). The stakeholder theory of the corporation: Concepts, evidence, and implications. *Academy of Management Review, 20*(1), 65–91. https://doi.org/10.5465/amr.1995.9503271992

dos Reis Cardillo, M. A., & Basso, L. F. C. (2025). Revisiting knowledge on ESG/CSR and financial performance: A bibliometric and systematic review of moderating variables. *Journal of Innovation & Knowledge, 10*(1), 100648. https://doi.org/10.1016/j.jik.2024.100648

Drempetic, S., Klein, C., & Zwergel, B. (2020). The influence of firm size on the ESG score: Corporate sustainability ratings under review. *Journal of Business Ethics, 167*, 333–360. https://doi.org/10.1007/s10551-019-04164-1

Dumitrescu, A., & Zakriya, M. (2021). Stakeholders and the stock price crash risk: What matters in corporate social performance? *Journal of Corporate Finance, 67*, 101871. https://doi.org/10.1016/j.jcorpfin.2020.101871

Dumrose, M., Rink, S., & Eckert, J. (2022). Disaggregating confusion? The EU Taxonomy and its relation to ESG rating. *Finance Research Letters, 48*, 102928. https://doi.org/10.1016/j.frl.2022.102928

Eberle, D., Berens, G., & Li, T. (2013). The impact of interactive corporate social responsibility communication on corporate reputation. *Journal of Business Ethics, 118*(4), 731–746. https://doi.org/10.1007/s10551-013-1957-y

Ehlers, T., Packer, F., & De Greiff, K. (2022). The pricing of carbon risk in syndicated loans: Which risks are priced and why? *Journal of Banking & Finance, 136*, 106180. https://doi.org/10.1016/j.jbankfin.2021.106180

El Ghoul, S., Guedhami, O., Kwok, C. C. Y., & Mishra, D. R. (2011). Does corporate social responsibility affect the cost of capital? *Journal of Banking & Finance, 35*(9), 2388–2406. https://doi.org/10.1016/j.jbankfin.2011.02.007

ElTarabishy, A., & Baldegger, R. (2024). *Global micro-, small and medium-sized enterprises report.* International Council for Small Business.

Endrikat, J., Guenther, E., & Hoppe, H. (2014). Making sense of conflicting empirical findings: A meta-analytic review of the relationship between corporate environmental and financial performance. *European Management Journal, 32*(5), 735–751. https://doi.org/10.1016/j.emj.2013.12.004

Evans, W. M., & Freeman, R. E. (1988). A stakeholder theory of the modern corporation: Kantian capitalism. In *T. L. Beauchamp, & N. E. Bowie (Eds.), Ethical theory and business* (pp. 75–93). Prentice Hall.

Fard, A., Javadi, S., & Kim, I. (2020). Environmental regulation and the cost of bank loans: International evidence. *Journal of Financial Stability, 51*, 100797. https://doi.org/10.1016/j.jfs.2020.100797

Fombrun, C. J., Gardberg, N. A., & Barnett, M. L. (2000). Opportunity platforms and safety nets: Corporate citizenship and reputational risk. *Business and Society Review, 105*(1), 85–106. https://doi.org/10.1111/0045-3609.00066

Forcadell, F. J., & Aracil, E. (2017). European banks' reputation for corporate social responsibility. *Corporate Social Responsibility and Environmental Management, 24*(1), 1–14. https://doi.org/10.1002/csr.1392

Freeman, R. E. (1984). *Strategic management: A stakeholder approach.* Pitman.

Freeman, R. E., Dmytriyev, S. D., & Phillips, R. A. (2021). Stakeholder theory and the resource-based view of the firm. *Journal of Management, 47*(7), 1757–1770. https://doi.org/10.1177/0149206321993576

Freeman, R. E., Wicks, A. C., & Parmar, B. (2004). Stakeholder theory and "the corporate objective revisited." *Organization Science, 15*(3), 364–369. https://doi.org/10.1287/orsc.1040.0066

Friede, G., Busch, T., & Bassen, A. (2015). ESG and financial performance: Aggregated evidence from more than 2000 empirical studies. *Journal of Sustainable Finance & Investment, 5*(4), 210–233. https://doi.org/10.1080/20430795.2015.1118917

Friedman, M. (1970, September 13). The social responsibility of business is to increase its profits. *The New York Times Magazine*, 32–33.

Friedman, M. (2007). The social responsibility of business is to increase its profits. In *G. G. Brenkert, & T. L. Beauchamp (Eds.), Corporate ethics and corporate governance* (pp. 173–178). Springer.

Gao-Zeller, X., Li, X., Yang, F., & Zhu, W. (2019). Driving mechanism of CSR strategy in Chinese construction companies based on neo-institutional theory. *KSCE Journal of Civil Engineering, 23*(5), 1939–1951. https://doi.org/10.1007/s12205-019-1974-9

Gholami, A., Murray, P. A., & Sands, J. (2022). Environmental, social, governance & financial performance disclosure for large firms: Is this different for SME firms? *Sustainability, 14*(10), 6019. https://doi.org/10.3390/su14106019

Gibson Brandon, R., Krueger, P., & Schmidt, P. S. (2021). ESG rating disagreement and stock returns. *Financial Analysts Journal, 77*(4), 104–127.

Giese, G., Lee, L. E., Melas, D., Nagy, Z., & Nishikawa, L. (2019). Foundations of ESG investing: How ESG affects equity valuation, risk, and performance. *The Journal of Portfolio Management, 45*(5), 69–83. https://doi.org/10.3905/jpm.2019.45.5.069

Gislain, J. J. (2002). Causalité institutionnelle: La futurité chez J. R. Commons. *Économie et Institutions, 1*, 47–66.

Gjergji, R., Vena, L., Sciascia, S., & Cortesi, A. (2021). The effects of environmental, social and governance disclosure on the cost of capital in small and medium enterprises: The role of family business status. *Business Strategy and the Environment, 30*(1), 683–693. https://doi.org/10.1002/bse.2647

Golrida, K., Bambang, S., Sutrisno, T., & Erwin, S. (2020). Explaining the complexity relationship of CSR and financial performance using neo-institutional theory. *Journal of Asian Business and Economic Studies, 27*(3), 227–244. https://doi.org/10.1108/JABES-03-2020-0026

Habermas, J. (1978). *Raison et légitimité* (J. Coste, Trans.). Payot.

Habib, A. M., & Mourad, N. (2024). The influence of environmental, social, and governance (ESG) practices on US firms' performance: Evidence from the coronavirus crisis. *Journal of the Knowledge Economy, 15*(1), 2549–2570.

Hahn, T., Figge, F., Pinkse, J., & Preuss, L. (2018). A paradox perspective on corporate sustainability: Descriptive, instrumental, and normative aspects. *Journal of Business Ethics, 148*(2), 235–248.

Hart, S. L. (1995). A natural-resource-based view of the firm. *Academy of Management Review, 20*(4), 986–1014.

Hatch, M. J. (2000). *Théorie des organisations: De l'intérêt des perspectives multiples.* De Boeck Université.

Hopner, A. G. F., Yu, P. S., & Ferguson, J. (2010). Corporate social responsibility across industries: When can who do well by doing good? *SSRN Electronic Journal.* https://doi.org/10.2139/ssrn.3025993

Javadi, S., & Masum, A. A. (2021). The impact of climate change on the cost of bank loans. *Journal of Corporate Finance, 69*, 102019.

Jawahar, I. M., & McLaughlin, G. L. (2001). Toward a descriptive stakeholder theory: An organizational life cycle approach. *Academy of Management Review, 26*(3), 397–414.

Jones, T. M. (1995). Instrumental stakeholder theory: A synthesis of ethics and economics. *Academy of Management Review, 20*(2), 404–437.

Kaler, J. (2003). Differentiating stakeholder theories. *Journal of Business Ethics, 46*(1), 71–83.

Kim, J., & Park, T. (2020). How corporate social responsibility (CSR) saves a company: The role of gratitude in buffering vindictive consumer behavior from product failures. *Journal of Business Research, 117*, 461–472.

King, A. A., & Lenox, M. J. (2002). Exploring the locus of profitable pollution reduction. *Management Science, 48*(2), 289–299.

King, A. A., Lenox, M. J., & Terlaak, A. (2005). The strategic use of decentralized institutions: Exploring certification with the ISO 14001 management standard. *Academy of Management Journal, 48*(6), 1091–1106.

Kiymaz, H. (2012). SRI mutual fund and index performance. In T. Hebb, J. P. Hawley, A. G. F. Hoepner, A. L. Neher, & D. Wood (Eds.), *The Oxford handbook of socially responsible investing* (pp. 425–442). Oxford University Press. https://doi.org/10.1093/oxfordhb/9780199642823.013.0022

Kling, G., Volz, U., Murinde, V., & Ayas, S. (2021). The impact of climate vulnerability on firms' cost of capital and access to finance. *World Development, 137*, 105131.

Konar, S., & Cohen, M. A. (2001). Does the market value environmental performance? *Review of Economics and Statistics, 83*(2), 281–289.

Krüger, P. (2015). Corporate goodness and shareholder wealth. *Journal of Financial Economics, 115*(2), 304–329.

Kusumaningtias, R., Kamaluddin, A., Ismail, A. H., Alias, P., Venusita, L., & Putra, R. (2021). Accountability in SME Islamic entrepreneurship during the COVID-19 pandemic. *Management & Accounting Review, 20*(2), 161–178.

Lamertz, K., & Baum, J. A. C. (1998). The legitimacy of organizational downsizing in Canada: An analysis of explanatory media accounts. *Canadian Journal of Administrative Sciences, 15*(1), 93–107.

Lee, S. P., & Isa, M. (2023). Environmental, social and governance (ESG) practices and financial performance of Shariah-compliant companies in Malaysia. *Journal of Islamic Accounting and Business Research, 14*(2), 295–314.

Li, W., Yan, T., & Li, Y. (2025). Corporate social responsibility and financial performance in a cross-country context: A meta-analysis. *Journal of Business Research, 190*, 115218.

Li, Y., Gong, M., Zhang, X. Y., & Koh, L. (2018). The impact of environmental, social, and governance disclosure on firm value: The role of CEO power. *The British Accounting Review, 50*(1), 60–75.

Limkriangkrai, M., Koh, S., & Durand, R. B. (2017). Environmental, social, and governance (ESG) profiles, stock returns, and financial policy: Australian evidence. *International Review of Finance, 17*(3), 461–471.

Lépineux, F. (2003). *Dans quelle mesure une entreprise peut-elle être responsable à l'égard de la cohésion sociale?* (Doctoral dissertation, Conservatoire National des Arts et Métiers).

Lubin, D. A., & Esty, D. C. (2010). The sustainability imperative. *Harvard Business Review, 88*, 42–50.

MacNeil, I., & Esser, I. M. (2022). From a financial to an entity model of ESG. *European Business Organization Law Review, 23*(1), 9–45.

Margolis, J. D., & Walsh, J. P. (2003). Misery loves companies: Rethinking social initiatives by business. *Administrative Science Quarterly, 48*(2), 268–305.

Martinet, A. C., & Reynaud, E. (2015). Shareholders, stakeholders et stratégie. *Revue Française de Gestion, 253*(8), 297–317.

McWilliams, A., & Siegel, D. (2000). Corporate social responsibility and financial performance: Correlation or misspecification? *Strategic Management Journal, 21*(5), 603–609.

Meadows, D. H., Meadows, D. L., Randers, J., & Behrens, W. W., III. (1972). *The limits to growth: A report for the Club of Rome*. Universe Books.

Mercier, S. (1999). *L'éthique dans les entreprises*. La Découverte.

Meyer, J. W., & Rowan, B. (1977/1991). Institutionalized organizations: Formal structure as myth and ceremony. In W. W. Powell, & P. J. DiMaggio (Eds.), *The new institutionalism in organizational analysis* (pp. 41–62). University of Chicago Press.

Minutolo, M. C., Kristjanpoller, W. D., & Stakeley, J. (2019). Exploring environmental, social, and governance disclosure effects on the S&P 500 financial performance. *Business Strategy and the Environment, 28*(6), 1083–1095. https://doi.org/10.1002/bse.2303

Moneva, J. M., & Llena, F. (2000). Environmental disclosures in the annual reports of large companies in Spain. *European Accounting Review, 9*(1), 7–29. https://doi.org/10.1080/096381800407923

Nazari, J. A., Hrazdil, K., & Mahmoudian, F. (2017). Assessing social and environmental performance through narrative complexity in CSR reports. *Journal of Contemporary Accounting & Economics, 13*(2), 166–178.

Nirino, N., Santoro, G., Miglietta, N., & Quaglia, R. (2021). Corporate controversies and company's financial performance: Exploring the moderating role of ESG practices. *Technological Forecasting and Social Change, 162*, 120341. https://doi.org/10.1016/j.techfore.2020.120341

Porter, M. E., Serafeim, G., & Kramer, M. R. (2019, October 16). Where ESG fails. *Institutional Investor*.

Reinhardt, F. L. (1999). Bringing the environment down to earth. *Harvard Business Review, 77*(4), 149–157.

Ruef, M., & Scott, W. R. (1998). A multidimensional model of organizational legitimacy: Hospital survival in changing institutional environments. *Administrative Science Quarterly, 43*(4), 877–904. https://doi.org/10.2307/2393619

Russo, M. V., & Fouts, P. A. (1997). A resource-based perspective on corporate environmental performance and profitability. *Academy of Management Journal, 40*(3), 534–559. https://doi.org/10.2307/257052

Scott, W. R. (1995). *Institutions and organizations*. SAGE Publications.

Scott, W. R. (2001). *Institutions and organizations* (2nd ed.). SAGE Publications.

Selznick, P. (1949). *TVA and the grass roots: A study in the sociology of formal organization*. University of California Press.

Serafeim, G. (2020). Public sentiment and the price of corporate sustainability. *Financial Analysts Journal, 76*(2), 26–46. https://doi.org/10.1080/0015198X.2020.1730896

Spence, M. (1973). Job market signaling. *The Quarterly Journal of Economics, 87*(3), 355–374. https://doi.org/10.2307/1882010

Stiglitz, J. E. (2000). The contributions of the economics of information to twentieth century economics. *The Quarterly Journal of Economics, 115*(4), 1441–1478. https://doi.org/10.1162/003355300555015

Stone, M. M., & Brush, C. G. (1996). Planning in ambiguous contexts: The dilemma of meeting needs for commitment and demands for legitimacy. *Strategic Management Journal, 17*(8), 633–652. https://doi.org/10.1002/(SICI)1097-0266(199610)17:8<633::AID-SMJ832>3.0.CO;2-V

Su, W., Peng, M. W., Tan, W., & Cheung, Y. L. (2016). The signaling effect of corporate social responsibility in emerging economies. *Journal of Business Ethics, 134*(3), 479–491. https://doi.org/10.1007/s10551-014-2424-4

Suchman, M. C. (1995). Managing legitimacy: Strategic and institutional approaches. *Academy of Management Review, 20*(3), 571–610. https://doi.org/10.5465/amr.1995.9508080331

Weber, M. (1971). *Économie et société* (Vol. 1). Plon.

Wei, W., Kim, G., Miao, L., Behnke, C., & Almanza, B. (2018). Consumer inferences of corporate social responsibility (CSR) claims on packaged foods. *Journal of Business Research, 83*, 186–201. https://doi.org/10.1016/j.jbusres.2017.10.040

Yoon, B., & Chung, Y. (2018). The effects of corporate social responsibility on firm performance: A stakeholder approach. *Journal of Hospitality and Tourism Management, 37*, 89–96. https://doi.org/10.1016/j.jhtm.2018.10.005

Zimmerman, M. A., & Zeitz, G. J. (2002). Beyond survival: Achieving new venture growth by building legitimacy. *Academy of Management Review, 27*(3), 414–431. https://doi.org/10.5465/amr.2002.7389921

CHAPTER 4

ESG Analysis: Methodological Approach for the Calculation of a Composite Indicator

Sandra Kendo, Qing Xu, Ivan Terraglia, and Oussama Kacemi

Abstract This chapter operationalizes the ESG conceptual and regulatory foundations discussed in earlier chapters by proposing a structured methodology to calculate a composite ESG indicator. It responds to the persistent challenge of standardization in ESG measurement and the need for robust tools to assess corporate sustainability in a coherent, comparable manner. Recognizing the inconsistencies among ESG rating agencies, the chapter builds on existing literature and empirical critiques to construct a transparent and theoretically grounded indicator based on the Mazziotta-Pareto Index (MPI), a non-compensatory aggregation method.

The proposed composite indicator evaluates ESG performance across SMEs' three traditional pillars (Environmental, Social, and Governance).

S. Kendo • Q. Xu (✉) • O. Kacemi
ICL, Junia, Université Catholique de Lille, LITL
e-mail: qing.xu@univ-catholille.fr

I. Terraglia
University of Teramo, Italia

S. Kendo (ed.), *Non-Financial Reporting and ESG Performance*, Palgrave Studies in Impact Finance,
https://doi.org/10.1007/978-3-032-19092-5_4

This design ensures that weaknesses in one ESG domain cannot be masked by strengths in another, preserving the integrity of multi-dimensional sustainability assessment.

The chapter also outlines the challenges posed by divergent ESG rating methodologies, emphasizing the impact of measurement, scope, and weighting discrepancies. It reviews major rating systems (Bloomberg, MSCI, Sustainalytics, Refinitiv, ISS).

Keywords ESG Composite Index • Ratings • PCA • SMEs

4.1 Introduction

Based on the studies previously mentioned, this chapter aims to propose a robust methodology for calculating an ESG sustainability indicator for small and medium companies and examining its relations with their financial performance. Recent literature has long sought to address the issue of standardization in ESG measurement and its relationship with corporate financial variables (Dorfleitner et al., 2015). An increasing number of rating agencies and standard setters are exploring non-financial performance indicators; however, a unified definition has yet to be established, likely due to the numerous complexities inherent in this field, particularly concerning the various industrial sectors that make up the global economy (Escrig-Olmedo et al., 2019). The only widely accepted definition categorizes corporate sustainability non-financial indicators into three pillars: Environmental (E), Social (S), and Governance (G), as illustrated in general terms in Fig. 4.1. In addition to these, so-called controversial ESG criteria exist—indicators that, despite being included in sustainability assessments, raise concerns regarding their coherence and effectiveness. For instance, companies operating in sectors such as nuclear energy or oil may receive high ESG scores, despite the environmental impact of their activities, due to improvements in risk management. Similarly, firms operating in countries with questionable ethical standards may still receive positive evaluations. Furthermore, ESG finance is often accused of greenwashing, as some supposedly sustainable funds include companies with questionable environmental, social, and governance practices. These aspects highlight the need for greater transparency and standardization (Aouadi & Marsat, 2018).

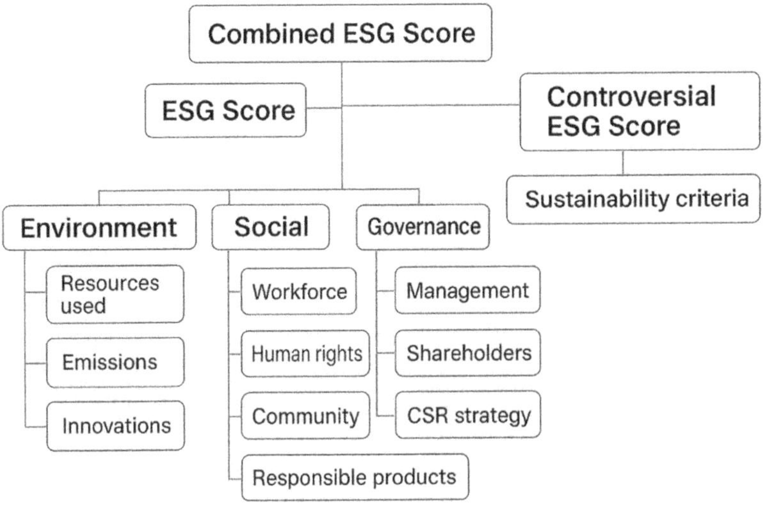

Fig. 4.1 ESG Score. Source: Authors

To compare the ESG performance of each company included in this study, a composite indicator will be calculated within the three ESG pillars. The methodology adopted, the Mazziotta-Pareto Index (MPI), is a non-compensatory aggregation method, meaning that deficiencies in one indicator cannot be offset by superior performance in others (Mazziotta & Pareto, 2022). This characteristic ensures that weaknesses in one aspect of sustainability are not masked by strengths in another, thus providing a more balanced and accurate assessment of a firm's ESG performance (Mazziotta & Pareto, 2012; Cerciello et al., 2023; Agnese et al., 2025). The calculation process will be conducted stepwise. First, individual indicators will be computed for each of the three ESG dimensions: an Environmental indicator (E), a Social indicator (S), and a Governance indicator (G). Each of these indicators will be derived by applying the MPI methodology, which standardizes and normalizes data while preserving the original distribution of values, thereby ensuring comparability across firms and industries. Once the three pillar-specific indicators have been obtained, they will be aggregated using a weighted mean to generate a final comprehensive ESG index. This approach enables an overall assessment while preserving the integrity of the individual dimensions, ensuring that each component of sustainability—environmental responsibility, social impact, and corporate governance—is adequately represented in the final measure.

4.2 The Challenge of Standardization in ESG Measurement

Over the last decade, investors have shown a growing interest in the ESG performance of companies. By July 7, 2025, 5,180 organizations (investment managers, asset owners, and service providers) had signed on to the Principles for Responsible Investment, reflecting the growing global commitment to sustainable and responsible finance (Principles for Responsible Investment, 2025). As a result, ESG ratings are increasingly utilized in asset management and academic research, and several ESG rating systems have emerged (Berg et al., 2022).

Despite the growing importance of ESG ratings and the increasing number of investors and corporate decision-makers relying on a company's ESG performance, one of the key challenges to overcome has been the divergent nature of ESG ratings among major rating institutions (Dimson, 2020). Chatterji et al. (2016) demonstrate that different evaluators do not necessarily agree on what constitutes corporate social responsibility, which they refer to as "theorizing"; however, they may end up measuring the same indicator (i.e., "commensurability") differently. Berg et al. (2022) provide further evidence, showing that measurement divergence is the primary driver of overall disagreement on ESG factors, accounting for 56% of the variation, while scope divergence (disagreement on the appropriate attributes of ESG factors) accounts for 38% of the variation. They also find a small but significant effect of different weighting systems on ESG rating divergence. The research also documents a rating institution effect, as well as a rated company effect. Berg et al. (2022) find that the rating institution is the main explanatory factor for measurement divergence. Christensen et al. (2022) present evidence that the more ESG information a company discloses, the greater the divergence in ESG ratings.

Disagreement on ESG ratings can have significant consequences, as it can make it more difficult for asset managers to select appropriate investment opportunities, which in turn can affect companies' cost of capital. Gibson Brandon et al. (2021) find that stock returns are positively associated with disagreement over ESG ratings, suggesting a higher risk premium for companies with greater disagreement over ESG performance. Although it is challenging to reconcile disagreements over the definition, the measurement and the weighting of the various ESG factors, the EU (European Union) taxonomy, which aims to develop a classification system for sustainable economic activities, could potentially solve the problem: the results of Dumrose et al. (2022) indicate that three of the four ESG rating systems are closely associated with the EU taxonomy.

4.2.1 The ESG Rating Agencies

ESG rating agencies evaluate a company's ESG performance to provide investors and stakeholders with an assessment of its sustainability practices and associated ESG risks. These agencies examine factors such as carbon emissions, diversity and inclusion policies, board composition, labor practices, supply chain management, and corporate governance structures. The ratings may play a crucial role in helping investors make informed decisions, considering both a company's financial performance and its impact on society and the environment. Bloomberg, MSCI, Sustainalytics (Morningstar), Refinitiv, and ISS (Deutsche) are the major rating agencies. These agencies use different methodologies and data sources to evaluate ESG factors and produce ratings or scores that investors can use to assess a company's sustainability profile, as described in Annex 1.

Bloomberg ESG scores (Bloomberg, 2025) measure a company's management of ESG issues that could impact its financial performance, including revenue streams, operating costs, cost of capital, and asset and liability values. Bloomberg ratings are based on publicly available company data and peer group comparisons (same industry, similar business model, and similar ESG risks and opportunities). Bloomberg ESG Scores consider the disclosure of quantitative data as a dimension of performance. These scores range from 0 to 10, with higher scores indicating better management of material issues. The global ESG score assesses a company's aggregate ESG performance across the E, S, and G pillars. The weighting of the pillars depends on the financial significance of each one.

MSCI ESG Ratings (MSCI, 2025) utilize three pillars (E, S, G), ten themes, and 33 ESG key issues to assess companies' ESG risk exposure and management capabilities related to financially relevant ESG risks and opportunities, ultimately identifying industry leaders and laggards among peers. MSCI ESG Ratings range from leader (AAA, AA), average (A, BBB, BB), to laggard (B, CCC).

Morningstar Sustainalytics' ESG Risk Rating (Morningstar Sustainalytics, 2024) assesses the extent to which ESG factors threaten a company's economic value (or enterprise value). These ratings determine the gap in unmanaged ESG risks by analyzing Material ESG Issues, based on the company's exposure to these issues and its management thereof. Individual unmanaged risks are then aggregated into a single score representing the company's overall ESG risk. Sustainalytics' ESG risk ratings are based on three key elements that contribute to a company's overall rating: (1) Material ESG issues: These include the environmental, social, and governance aspects that are most relevant to the company and its sector of activity; (2) The quality of corporate governance and stakeholder management; and (3) Systemic and idiosyncratic ESG issues: Systemic issues refer to ESG risks affecting the entire sector or economy, while idiosyncratic issues concern risks specific to the company.

The LSEG (Refinitiv) ESG scores (Refinitiv, 2022; LSEG, 2024) are designed to provide a transparent and objective measure of a company's performance in environmental, social, and governance (ESG) criteria, as well as its commitment and effectiveness, based on data provided by the company itself. These scores cover ten main themes. The LSEG also offers a combined global ESG score, which incorporates significant ESG controversies that may affect the companies covered.

ISS's ESG corporate ratings (ISS ESG, 2023; ISS ESG 2024) are designed to enable institutional investors to support their investment strategies by assessing the environmental, social, and governance (ESG) performance of investee companies. ESG performance refers to a company's ability to effectively manage significant ESG risks, mitigate negative social and environmental impacts, generate positive impacts, and capitalize on the opportunities presented by the transition to sustainable development. ISS ESG recognizes that each business model presents a unique set of risks, opportunities, and impacts. To capture and reflect these characteristics, a specific approach is implemented for each sector and sub-sector through a proprietary classification system. The ESG rating of companies consists of two main dimensions: (1) the social and governance dimension, and (2) the environmental dimension. Each dimension is then subdivided into three categories, which are further broken down into themes and indicators, located at different levels of the rating hierarchy. Weightings for themes and indicators are assigned at each level of the hierarchy, for example, dimension, category, theme, and indicator.

4.2.2 Core ESG Factors and Their Components

The ESG framework provides a comprehensive tool for assessing corporate sustainability performance, structured around three fundamental pillars.

From an environmental perspective, the analysis focuses on the company's overall ecological footprint. This includes a detailed assessment of energy management, examining both total consumption and the proportion of renewable energy sources. Water policy is scrutinized through conservation strategies and water recycling initiatives. The carbon footprint receives particular attention, with an analysis of greenhouse gas emissions, offset measures, and reduction programs. Digital transformation is considered a key lever for environmental optimization, particularly through the use of smart energy management systems. Circular economy practices and responsible sourcing within the value chain are evaluated, along with procedures for managing hazardous materials and waste.

The social dimension evaluates the company's commitment to its human capital and its impact on the broader societal environment. Local partnerships and territorial integration demonstrate the company's deep-seated connection to its regional ecosystem. Employment policies are analyzed in terms of job stability, pay equity, and workforce diversity. Working conditions are examined through the lens of occupational risk prevention and compliance with safety standards. Workplace well-being is evaluated through specific programs, including quality-of-life initiatives and work-life balance. Skills development and career progression opportunities complete this thorough social analysis.

The governance component measures the quality of decision-making structures and managerial ethics. Wealth distribution is analyzed, particularly through the study of pay gaps and redistribution policies. Employee representation in governance bodies and gender parity in decision-making organs receive special attention. The degree of decentralization and organizational transparency serves as an indicator of governance maturity. CSR (Corporate Social Responsibility) policy is examined holistically, incorporating both ethical aspects and sustainability commitments. Finally, consumer protection (product safety, commercial practices) and rigorous supplier selection, based on ethical and environmental criteria complete this evaluation triad.

This multidimensional analytical grid enables a nuanced and balanced assessment of corporate sustainability performance, systematically integrating environmental impacts, social responsibilities, and governance quality. The framework's strength lies in its ability to capture the complex interconnections between ecological preservation, social equity, and ethical management practices, providing stakeholders with a robust tool for informed decision-making. By maintaining this comprehensive approach, the ESG model continues to evolve as the gold standard for measuring and comparing corporate sustainability across industries and regions.

4.3 Methodology for Constructing the Composite ESG Indicator

4.3.1 Composite Index Construction

This study focuses on developing a synthetic indicator to measure and compare corporate ESG accounting data in a standardized way. A composite index is proposed as a practical solution because it combines multiple individual indicators into a single metric, capturing different dimensions of a complex concept—in this case, corporate sustainability and non-financial performance. Such indices are particularly useful when no single indicator can fully represent the phenomenon under analysis (OECD, 2008).

The construction of a composite index requires a structured methodological approach, grounded in a theoretical framework that defines the phenomenon being measured. This framework guides the selection of relevant indicators, their normalization, weighting, and aggregation. The selection of elementary indicators is crucial, as the reliability of the composite index depends on the quality of these underlying variables. Given that the data comes from a survey of enterprises, the model is formative—meaning each indicator contributes independently to the overall construct rather than reflecting a single latent trait.

Before aggregation, normalization is necessary to ensure comparability among indicators, which may have different units or scales. Standard normalization techniques include Min-Max scaling (adjusting values to a 0–1 range), z-score standardization (expressing data in terms of standard deviations from the mean), and rank transformation. The choice of method depends on data characteristics and can influence the final results.

The aggregation step involves combining normalized indicators into a single index, which requires decisions on weighting (e.g., equal weights versus expert-based weights) and the selection of an appropriate aggregation method. Two main approaches exist:

- Compensatory aggregation (e.g., arithmetic mean), where high performance in one indicator can offset low performance in another.
- Non-compensatory aggregation, where imbalances between indicators are penalized, ensuring no single dimension is overlooked.

Finally, the composite index must undergo validation to confirm its reliability and usefulness. This involves assessing robustness (stability under different methodological choices) and discriminatory power (the ability to differentiate between companies effectively). A well-validated index provides a consistent and meaningful tool for evaluating and comparing corporate ESG performance.

By following this structured process, the study aims to create a transparent, theoretically grounded, and empirically sound ESG measurement tool for businesses and stakeholders.

4.3.2 The Mazziotta & Pareto Index

Given the nature of simple indicators, a non-compensatory aggregation methodology was chosen to ensure that each value of any variable included in the calculation is adequately considered and retains its significance (Mazziotta & Pareto, 2013).

The penalty method based on the coefficient of variation, also known as the Mazziotta-Pareto Index (MPI), enables the construction of a synthetic measure of ESG performances in Hauts-de-France firms, under the assumption that each component is either non-substitutable or only partially substitutable (De Muro et al., 2012). This non-compensatory approach requires a balanced distribution of all elementary components. The resulting index is constructed based on several key principles. First, the standardization of indicators is achieved through a transformation process that eliminates both unit dependence and variability, ensuring greater comparability across different measures. Moreover, the approach is designed to maintain computational simplicity while ensuring that the final index remains easy to interpret and apply in various analytical contexts.

These requirements are met by standardizing indicators as normalized deviations, ensuring comparability despite differences in measurement scales. Each indicator is transformed into a standardized variable with a mean of 100 and a standard deviation of 10, constraining values approximately within the range 70–130. Unlike methods relying on predefined target values, this approach anchors comparisons to the empirical mean, allowing for a straightforward identification of units with above-average (> 100) or below-average (< 100).

Equation 1

$$\mathrm{z_{ij}} = 100 \pm \frac{(x_{ij} - M_{x_j})}{S_{x_j}} 10$$

Where:

- x_{ij} is the raw value of the observation for individual i in variable j,
- z_{ij} is the standardized value of x_{ij},
- M_{x_j} is the arithmetic mean of the variable,
- S_{x_j} is the standard deviation of the variable,
- 100 is the mean of the standardized scale,
- 10 is the scaling factor to adjust the standard deviation.

In the equation, the sign will depend on the relationship—whether positive or negative—of the individual variable in the calculation of the indicator.

To refine the aggregation function (arithmetic mean of standardized variables), a penalty coefficient is introduced, accounting for horizontal variability—the dispersion of indicators around the mean. The coefficient of variation adjusts the scores of units exhibiting greater imbalances, thus mitigating distortions caused by asymmetric distributions of single components.

Equation 2

$$cv_i = \frac{S_{z_i}}{M_{z_i}}$$

Where:

- cv_i is the coefficient of variation of the standardized variables for individual i,
- S_{z_i} is the standard deviation of the standardized variables for individual i,
- M_{z_i} is the arithmetic mean of the standardized variables for individual i.

Finally, the use of standardized deviations enhances the robustness of the synthetic index, minimizing sensitivity to the exclusion of individual indicators.

Equation 3

$$MPI_I^{+/-} = M_{z_i} \pm S_{z_i} cv_i$$

Where:

- $MPI_I^{+/-}$ is the the aggregated score for a single dimension (E, S, or G) for individual i,
- M_{z_i} is the arithmetic mean of the standardized variables for individual i,
- S_{z_i} is the standard deviation of the standardized variables for individual i,
- cv_i is the coefficient of variation of the standardized variables for individual i.

The $\pm$ sign varies depending on the nature of the phenomenon under consideration and, consequently, on the direction of the elementary indicators. When the indicator is increasing or positive, meaning that higher values correspond to a positive effect on the phenomenon, a negative penalty is applied. Conversely, when the indicator is decreasing or negative, implying that higher values indicate a worsening condition, a positive penalty is used. In the first case, the penalty coefficient adjusts the mean of the standardized indicators by lowering it, whereas in the second case, it acts in the opposite direction, raising the mean. In this study, we adopt the version with a negative penalty, because the indicators have a positive effect on the final result.

Equation 4

$$MPI_I^- = M_{z_i} - S_{z_i} cv_i$$

After that, all the single dimensions of the ESG indicator will be aggregated by a weighted mean to create the final indicator of non-financial sustainability performance. The weighting system applied will be the one adopted by Bloomberg's rating agency for its ESG index. This methodology assigns a score ranging from 1 to 5 to each of the three dimensions that constitute the multidimensional ESG framework, depending on their relevance to the sector in which the company operates. Subsequently, based on the assigned score, a percentage of importance is calculated, representing the weight of each dimension within the overall index.

Equation 5

$$MPI_{ESG_i} = \frac{MPI_{E_i} w_E + MPI_{S_i} w_S + MPI_{G_i} w_G}{\sum w}$$

Where:

- MPI_{ESG_i} is the final result of the Mazziotta-Pareto Index, after the aggregation of the three dimensions,
- MPI_{E_i} is the Mazziotta-Pareto Index for the environmental dimension,
- w_E is the weight assigned to the environmental indicator,
- MPI_{S_i} is the Mazziotta-Pareto Index for the social dimension,
- w_S is the weight assigned to the social indicator,
- MPI_{G_i} is the Mazziotta-Pareto Index for the governance dimension,
- w_G is the weight assigned to the governance indicator.

To ensure the reliability of the composite indicator, both robustness and sensitivity analyses will be conducted. Robustness will be assessed by developing a principal component analysis to better identify the most relevant components to include in the calculation of MPI.

Moreover, we will calculating the correlation between the three ESG dimensions and the final composite indicator. A strong and consistent correlation among these dimensions would indicate that no single component disproportionately influences the overall score, ensuring a balanced representation of the underlying factors.

Sensitivity, on the other hand, will be evaluated by examining the correlation between each variable and the composite indicator of the corresponding dimension. This analysis will help determine the extent to which each variable contributes to the aggregated score. Higher correlations will indicate a more substantial influence of a given variable within its respective dimension, whereas lower correlations may suggest a lesser impact or potential redundancy.

4.3.3 *Description of the Process for Selecting ESG Variables for SMEs*

SMEs, including VSEs, represent 99% of EU businesses and face distinct constraints in implementing ESG practices, which calls for tailored and proportionate extra-financial frameworks. The Corporate Sustainability Reporting Directive (CSRD) provides a common sustainability reference, while underscoring the importance of adapting ESG indicators to the operational realities of SMEs (Small, and Medium-sized Enterprises).

Selecting extra-financial variables for SMEs is critical to constructing a reliable ESG indicator that is both adapted to the operational realities of small businesses and aligned with international sustainability frameworks, notably the United Nations SDGs.

The objective is to propose a common reference framework of extra-financial measures, adapted to the realities of SMEs, that contributes to collective sustainable development goals, enables the calibration of ESG investment while accounting for potentially diminishing returns, and integrates the dimensions of intentionality and additionality. More broadly, this framework seeks to enhance comparability and transparency by establishing a common basis for analysis, thereby promoting a more sustainable ecosystem and a more reliable ESG metric.

The selection of extra-financial variables builds on initial empirical work conducted with our partner, "*Autonomie et Solidarité*" (A&S), a private equity firm supporting SMEs, ensuring that the proposed framework reflects practical and operational realities. A key methodological challenge identified at this stage concerned the linearization of the Environmental, Social and Governance (ESG) variables to be considered, to allow comparable analyses across SMEs. As mentioned earlier, we first examined the various existing ESG measures, as well as the rating approaches proposed by non-financial rating agencies and European directives, in particular via EFRAG (European Financial Reporting Advisory Group) and CSRD (Corporate Sustainability Reporting Directive).

The majority of the companies surveyed expressed difficulty navigating the multiplicity of existing reference systems. Based on this observation, prospecting was conducted to identify the real needs of SME managers regarding ESG, as well as their short- and medium-term objectives, with a view to developing the business and securing its stability and financial viability.

Based on the initial feedback from the field, several themes of interest have emerged concerning non-financial information, in particular:

- Governance Prospecting Issues: Membership of the SSE; number of women in leadership.
- Prospecting questions related to the social objective: Number of sustainable jobs created; inclusion and equality (number of workers benefiting from the Recognition of Disabled Worker Status (RQTH)); health and safety (absenteeism and turnover); quality-of-life at work (managerial practices that encourage listening and support); territorial development (establishment in rural areas or priority districts); stakeholders (CSR, commitment of suppliers).
- Environmental Objective Issues: Recycling (waste and effluent management); reduction of pollution (carbon footprint linked to employee mobility); Production (implementation of eco-design approaches).

The questionnaire has therefore been reworked to propose a common reference system of variables, easily understandable and readily mobilized by SMEs. The selection of these variables, inspired by rating agencies and European directives, was defined and finalized based mainly on the Sustainable Development Goals (SDGs). This choice allows for consistency in international comparisons while integrating a weighting that accounts for the usefulness and importance of macroeconomic activity.

The use of the SDGs aims to ensure cross-cutting use of the indicators, both within the European Union, in line with European directives, and in countries outside the European Union, in line with the Sustainable Development Goals defined by the United Nations (UN). On this basis, three ESG dimensions for SMEs are structured according to the following SDGs (Table 4.1).

Table 4.1 Alignment of ESG indicators with SDGs for SMEs

ESG Dimension	*SDG*	*Focus area*
i. Environmental dimension	SDG 12	Digital transformation.
	SDG 6	Water consumption.
	SDG 11	Carbon footprint.
ii. Social dimension	SDG 8	Sustainable employment.
	SDG 4	Human Capital Development.
iii. Governance dimension	SDG 16.7	Decentralization and employee representativeness.
	SDGs 12.6 and 12.8	CSR, supplier selection criteria, training and information.

Source: Authors.

This work has led to an ESG indicator adapted to the realities of SMEs, structured according to three levels of priorities:

- Level 1: concrete and easily measurable indicators based on available data (e.g., invoices, human resources data);
- Level 2: relevant indicators requiring methodological support for calculations (e.g., GHG emissions, water consumption); and
- Level 3: qualitative or less frequently documented indicators, but essential for the CSR strategy (e.g., well-being at work, stakeholder involvement).

Table 4.2 presents the key variables selected for each ESG dimension.

i. **Environmental dimension**: The variables were designed to measure the environmental impact of SMEs and were defined based on field surveys, with examples of questions capturing information both qualitatively and quantitatively.
ii. **Social dimension:** The proposed variables make it possible to evaluate working conditions, diversity and the quality of internal dialogue.
iii. **Governance dimension:** The variables identified reflect governance patterns, decision-making processes, transparency and ethics. These variables serve as the foundation for the scoring system and subsequent aggregation into the composite ESG indicator.

Table 4.2 Descriptive statistics of extra-financial indicators used for MPI aggregation

ESG dimension	*Variable*	*Example question*	*Impact*
i. Environmental dimension $(\text{MPI}_{\text{E}_i}, \text{w}_\text{E})$	Energy, climate and ecological transition (x_{i1}^1)	What is the share of renewable energy in your company's total energy consumption?	(+)
	Water and natural resources (x_{i1}^2)	Has the company implemented actions to reduce its water consumption?	(+)
	Sustainable mobility (x_{i1}^3)	Does the company have a mobility plan for commuting?	(+)
	Responsible digital (x_{i1}^4)	Has the company implemented measures to reduce its digital footprint?	(+)
	Waste and the circular economy (x_{i1}^k)	Does the company sort its waste? If so, which ones?	(+)
ii. Social dimension $(\text{MPI}_{\text{S}_i}, \text{w}_\text{S})$	Gender parity and employee participation (x_{i2}^1)	What is the percentage of women among the salaried workforce?	(+)
	Working conditions, health and well-being (x_{i2}^2)	Does the company have a psychosocial risk prevention program in place?	(+)
	Remuneration, equity and inclusion (x_{i2}^3)	Are actions put in place to guarantee equal pay between women and men?	(+)
	Sustainable employment (x_{i2}^4)	What is the percentage of permanent contracts (CDI) in your workforce?	(+)
	Social commitment and solidarity (x_{i2}^n)	Does the company participate in solidarity or sponsorship actions?	(+)
iii. Governance dimension $(\text{MPI}_{\text{G}_i}, \text{w}_\text{G})$	CSR strategy and integration of ESG issues (x_{i3}^1)	Are ESG issues integrated into the company's overall strategy?	(+)
	Stakeholders (x_{i3}^2)	Do you take your stakeholders' opinions into account?	(+)
	General financial indicators (x_{i3}^3)	Does the company track financial indicators related to CSR performance?	(+)
	Sustainable investments and financing	Do you have a dedicated budget for integrating ESG into your business plan?	(+)

Table 4.2 (continued)

ESG dimension	*Variable*	*Example question*	*Impact*
	Responsible suppliers and purchasing	Do you help your suppliers to implement at least one sustainable development approach?	(+)

Source: Authors.

The data collected from the questionnaire administered during the field survey enabled quantitative and qualitative information to be obtained. To integrate all this information into the proposed composite indicator as described in Section 3.2, a specific metric is applied to the qualitative variables. A scoring system on a scale of 0 to 5 is chosen for these variables.

Finally, given the limited volume of field data available at this stage, we have chosen to reduce the theoretical ambitions initially defined around the composite index and to propose, as a first step, a ranking-based approach, allowing us to initiate an initial exploratory analysis.

4.4 Statistical Analysis and ESG Composite Indicator

4.4.1 A Descriptive Statistical Analysis

The dataset contains 42 observations (SMEs) collected through a structured questionnaire covering the Environmental (E), Social (S), and Governance (G) pillars of ESG. The questionnaire includes 66 operational ESG variables usable for quantitative analysis, including binary items coded as 0/1, continuous variables (e.g., percentages or distances), and multi-response items transformed into counts of selected options.

Data were collected through multiple channels, including QR codes (5%), iframe-embedded questionnaires (2%), and direct administration (93%). The SMEs participating in the survey operate across different economic sectors, with manufacturing (24%), other service activities (22%), and wholesale and retail trade (15%) being the most represented. This sectoral diversity highlights the heterogeneity of business models and sustainability practices, supporting the use of a flexible ESG framework adapted to SMEs operating under varied economic and regulatory conditions. With regard to the governance dimension, the statistical results indicate that SMEs primarily associate ESG criteria with environmental practices, such as the reduction of greenhouse gas emissions (92.7%) and sustainable waste management (92.7%), as well as with social issues, notably gender parity (82.9%). A majority also recognize stakeholder dialogue (61%) as a relevant governance-related ESG criterion, reflecting an emerging awareness of participatory governance practices. However, with regard to the social dimension, only 48.8% of participants report regular collaboration or information exchange with civil society actors (associations, NGOs, etc.), while 51.2% indicate engagement in philanthropic or solidarity-based activities (e.g., sponsorship, donations, or local initiatives).

Among the environmental issues, waste sorting practices are universal, with 100% of surveyed SMEs reporting that they sort industrial and office waste. In addition, 92.7% of firms indicate that their workplace is accessible by public transport and/or bicycle, making these two items the most widely adopted environmental practices in the sample. Additonally, 90.2% of participants report that their company does not release polluting substances into the air, soil, or water, suggesting a low level of direct environmental pollution among the surveyed SMEs.

However, the results also reveal that 85.4% of participants do not communicate their carbon footprint to internal or external stakeholders, highlighting a gap between operational environmental practices and more strategic or transparency-oriented actions.

Table 4.3 summarizes the descriptive statistics of the variables used to construct the composite ESG indicators, including the number of observations, minimum and maximum values, and standard deviation for each variable. For selection-based questions (yes/no and multiple-choice items), responses are coded using binary indicators, with a value of 1 for "yes" and 0 for "no." Data are processed using Stata 17.

4.4.2 *The Composite ESG Indicator Calculation*

4.4.2.1 *The Z-Score Normalization and the Principal Component Analysis*

Step 1: Normalize the data using Z-Score as described in Section 3.2

Given the exploratory nature of this task, a subset of variables was selected just for testing in order to assess their contribution to, and impact on, the composite indicator. This step is essential, as the sign applied in the standardization procedure depends on the relationship, positive or

Table 4.3 Descriptive statistics of extra-financial indicators used for MPI aggregation[1]

ESG dimension	*Variable*	*Obs*	*Mean*	*Std. dev.*	*Min*	*Max*
Environmental dimension	e1	42	0.3571	0.4850	0	1
	e2	42	0.8810	0.3278	0	1
	e3	42	0.14286	0.3542	0	1
	e4	42	0.5952	0.4968	0	1
	e5	42	0.7857	0.4153	0	1
	e6	41	4.1463	17.4608	0	100
	e7	42	0.9048	0.2971	0	1
	e8	41	3.634146	15.7238	0	100
	e9	42	0.7619	0.4311	0	1
	e10	41	111,406.5	338,988.2	0	2,000,000
	e11	41	510,279	1,750,400	0	1.00E + 07
	e12	42	0.7619	0.4311	0	1
	e13	42	0.3095	0.4679	0	1
	e14	42	2.7381	0.9892	1	5
	e15	42	0.0952	0.2971	0	1
	e16	42	0.8333	0.3772	0	1
	e17	42	0.9762	0.1543	0	1
	e18	42	0.5	0.5061	0	1
	e19	42	0.6191	0.4915	0	1
Social dimension	s1	42	0.4762	0.5055	0	1
	s2	42	0.6429	0.4850	0	1
	s3	42	0.6667	0.4771	0	1
	s4	41	0.5518	0.2452	0.125	0.875
	s5	41	0.4878	1.4684	0	8
	s6	41	5,089.373	20,080.02	0	120,000
	s7	41	1.1220	1.3819	0	7
	s8	41	68.6585	45.6211	0	100
	s9	41	13.7561	11.4429	0	40
	s10	41	87.4390	31.6718	0	100
	s11	42	0.5952	0.4968	0	1
	s12	42	0.7857	0.4153	0	1
	s13	42	0.8333	0.3772	0	1
	s214	41	16.7072	103.9654	0	666
	s215	41	0.2927	1.5691	0	10
	s16	42	0.8571	0.3542	0	1
	s217	41	2.1707	4.7534	0	25
	s218	41	1.7317	3.9562	0	25
	s19	42	0.6905	0.4679	0	1
	s20	41	23.9756	68.8191	0	400
	s211	41	12.2195	32.0199	0	200
	s212	41	0.4146	1.0241	0	5
	s213	41	0.1707	0.5433	0	3

(continued)

Table 4.3 (continued)

ESG dimension	*Variable*	*Obs*	*Mean*	*Std. dev.*	*Min*	*Max*
	s214	41	16.7073	103.9654	0	666
	s215	41	0.2927	1.5691	0	10
	s216	41	17.7805	104.0628	0	666
	s217	41	2.1707	4.7534	0	25
	s218	41	1.7317	3.9562	0	25
	s22	41	17.1463	103.9104	0	666
	s23	41	19.5610	103.8583	0	666
	s24	42	0.5714	0.5009	0	1
	s25	42	0.3571	0.4850	0	1
Governance dimension	g1	42	3.3095	1.0238	1	4
	g2	41	16.1220	27.5093	0	100
	g3	41	18.6342	30.7423	0	100
	g4	42	2	1.4816	1	6
	g5	42	2.1429	1.6612	1	6
	g6	42	0.5476	0.5038	0	1
	g7	42	0.5476	0.5038	0	1
	g8	42	0.3809	0.4915	0	1
	g10	42	0.8571	0.3542	0	1
	g11	42	0.6429	0.4850	0	1
	g12	42	0.5952	0.4968	0	1
	g13	41	19.7561	26.3939	0	100
	g14	42	1.4048	0.4968	1	2
	g15	42	0.1190	0.3278	0	1
	g16	42	0.7381	0.4450	0	1
	g17	42	0.1191	0.3278	0	1
	g18	42	0.1191	0.3278	0	1
	g19	42	0.2143	0.4153	0	1
	g20	42	0.2857	0.4572	0	1
	g21	27	18,618.63	8,648.152	−21,549	24,112
	g22	42	0.6667	0.4771	0	1

Source: Authors.

[1] For the full definition of each variable for each pillar (environmental, social, and governance), please contact the authors. This was a highly dedicated study, and we would appreciate sharing this part, which was initially made available for free access.

negative, between each individual variable and the underlying sustainability dimension being measured (Table 4.4).

Step 2: PCA analysis

I. **Environmental PCA**

The results from the principal components/correlation (Table 4.5) indicate that the first principal component has an eigenvalue of 1.5916 and

Table 4.4 Descriptive statistics of z-score–standardized extra-financial indicators

ESG dimension	*Variable*	*Impact*	*Obs*	*Mean*	*Std. dev.*	*Min*	*Max*
Environmental dimension	z_e1	(+)	42	100	10	86.7443	107.3643
	z_e2	(+)	42	100	10	96.3680	126.8771
	z_e3	(+)	42	100	10	75.7985	104.0336
	z_e4	(+)	42	100	10	91.8526	111.9815
	z_e5	(+)	42	100	10	94.8402	118.9192
Social dimension	z_s1	(+)	42	100	10	89.6375	109.4204
	z_s2	(+)	42	100	10	92.6357	113.2557
	z_s3	(+)	42	100	10	93.0136	113.9728
	z_s4	(+)	41	100	9.9999	86.8217	117.4053
	z_s5	**(-)**	41	100	10	96.6779	151.1602
Governance dimension	z_g1	(+)	42	100	10	93.2559	122.558
	z_g2	(+)	41	100	9.9999	69.5092	105.8605
	z_g3	(+)	41	100	10	73.5329	106.0614
	z_g4	(+)	42	100	10	73.0021	106.7495
	z_g5	(+)	42	100	10	76.7810	106.8797

Source: Authors.

Table 4.5 Principal components/correlation for E

Component	*Eigenvalue*	*Difference*	*Proportion*	*Cumulative*
Comp1	1.5916	0.5123	0.3183	0.3183
Comp2	1.0791	0.1132	0.2158	0.5342
Comp3	0.9660	0.1408	0.1932	0.7274
Comp4	0.8253	0.2874	0.1651	0.8924
Comp5	0.5379	.	0.1076	1

Source: Authors.

explains 31.83% of the total variance, while the second component also slightly exceeds the Kaiser criterion, bringing cumulative explained variance to 53.42%. The first component is retained as the most representative latent environmental factor.

The eigenvector matrix (Table 4.6) shows that variables e2 and e4 exhibit the strongest positive loadings on the first component, indicating that they are the main contributors to the underlying environmental dimension. Overall, the PCA indicates a reasonable level of internal coherence among the environmental indicators and supports their aggregation within the composite ESG framework.

II. **Social PCA**

Similarly, the results from the principal components/correlation (Table 4.7) show that the first principal component has an eigenvalue of 1.7590 and explains 35.18% of the total variance, while the second component also exceeds the Kaiser criterion, bringing cumulative explained variance to 62.84%. Thus, the first component is retained as the latent social factor.

The eigenvector matrix (Table 4.8) indicates that variables s1 and s2 exhibit the strongest positive loadings on the first component, suggesting that they are key contributors to the latent social dimension. The remaining variables show more moderate or weaker loadings, reflecting heterogeneous social practices among SMEs. Overall, the PCA indicates a reasonable level of internal coherence among the social indicators and supports their aggregation within the composite ESG framework.

III. **Governance PCA**

The results from the principal components/correlation (Table 4.9) show that the first principal component has an eigenvalue of 2.27 and explains 45.4% of the total variance, while the second component also exceeds the Kaiser criterion, bringing cumulative explained variance up to 78.4%. This

Table 4.6 Principal components (eigenvectors) for E

Variable	*Comp1*	*Comp2*	*Comp3*	*Comp4*	*Comp5*
z_e1	0.2619	0.1236	0.9168	0.2748	-0.0089
z_e2	0.6335	0.0798	-0.0838	-0.3379	0.6864
z_e3	-0.0862	0.8235	-0.2272	0.476	0.1904
z_e4	0.6184	0.2697	-0.1727	-0.1568	-0.7003
z_e5	0.3746	-0.477	-0.2664	0.7477	0.0453

Source: Authors.

Table 4.7 Principal components/correlation for S

Component	*Eigenvalue*	*Difference*	*Proportion*	*Cumulative*
Comp1	1.7590	0.3759	0.3518	0.3518
Comp2	1.3831	0.4821	0.2766	0.6284
Comp3	0.9010	0.3068	0.1802	0.8086
Comp4	0.5942	0.2316	0.1188	0.9275
Comp5	0.3627	.	0.0725	1

Source: Authors.

Table 4.8 Principal components (eigenvectors) for S

Variable	*Comp1*	*Comp2*	*Comp3*	*Comp4*	*Comp5*
z_s1	0.5771	0.4028	0.1111	0.0082	0.7016
z_s2	0.5075	0.4963	-0.2179	-0.0595	-0.6672
z_s3	-0.443	0.4701	-0.1461	-0.7386	0.1263
z_s4	-0.3955	0.4539	-0.4602	0.6394	0.1302
z_s5	-0.2382	0.4055	0.8409	0.2052	-0.1725

Source: Authors.

Table 4.9 Principal components/correlation for G

Component	*Eigenvalue*	*Difference*	*Proportion*	*Cumulative*
Comp1	2.2720	0.6252	0.4544	0.4544
Comp2	1.6468	0.9446	0.3294	0.7838
Comp3	0.7022	0.4399	0.1404	0.9242
Comp4	0.2622	0.1454	0.0524	0.9766
Comp5	0.1168	.	0.0234	1

Source: Authors.

indicates the presence of a strong common governance factor among the selected indicators. So, the first component is retained as the latent governance factor.

The eigenvector matrix (Table 4.10) reveals that variables g4 and g5 load most strongly and positively on the first component, highlighting their central role in shaping governance performance among SMEs. The remaining variables exhibit more moderate contributions, reflecting heterogeneity in governance practices. Overall, the PCA indicates a reasonable level of internal coherence within the governance dimension and supports its aggregation within the composite ESG framework.

Across all three ESG dimensions, PCA reveals a dominant latent factor with coherent loadings, validating the aggregation of indicators into dimension-level scores and supporting the construction of a composite ESG indicator.

4.4.2.2 Derivation of a Composite Factor Based on the Outlined Methodology

Step 3: Calculating MPI for each dimension of ESG

The MPI for each dimension of ESG is calculated, and a summary of the results is presented in Table 4.11.

Table 4.10 Principal components (eigenvectors) for G

Variable	*Comp1*	*Comp2*	*Comp3*	*Comp4*	*Comp5*
z_g1	−0.2887	−0.424	0.8548	0.0778	0.0154
z_g2	−0.3784	0.5583	0.2113	−0.7012	0.0933
z_g3	−0.3003	0.629	0.1485	0.6969	−0.0801
z_g4	0.5876	0.2378	0.2984	0.0568	0.7113
z_g5	0.5814	0.2375	0.3371	−0.1152	−0.6919

Source: Authors.

Table 4.11 Summary on MPI of each dimension of ESG

Variable	*Obs*	*Mean*	*Std. dev.*	*Min*	*Max*
MPI_E	41	99.9116	5.2002	89.0275	113.7545
MPI_S	41	100.0345	5.4920	91.7167	112.1945
MPI_G	41	100.0266	4.8544	85.4645	111.9813

Source: Authors.

Step 4: Bloomberg weights
To simplify the calculations in this evaluation exercise, we assume that the weights assigned to the Environmental, Social, and Governance dimensions are broadly similar across economic sectors. In practice, however, these weights may vary significantly depending on sector-specific characteristics and sustainability priorities. Assuming that the importance of each ESG dimension is rated as reported in Table 4.12, the corresponding weights are calculated and presented in the rightmost column of the table.

Step 5: The composite ESG indicator
Fig. 4.2 (a)–(d) present the distributions of the MPI scores for the Environmental, Social, Governance dimensions and the overall ESG composite index. All distributions are approximately centered around the normalized mean value, indicating a reasonable spread of ESG performance among SMEs. Obviously, the skewness is observed in some dimensions, however no extreme outliers are detected, suggesting that the MPI produces stable and suitable for comparative analysis.

According to the MPI composite index, five of 42 firms achieved a high ranking of 1–5. Many firms in the sample should reevaluate their processes to improve their rankings toward the top ten. Notable progress has been

Table 4.12 Bloomberg weights for each dimension of ESG

ESG dimension	*Importance (1 = highest)*	*Weight*
E	4	20.0%
S	1	50.0%
G	3	30.0%

Source: Authors.

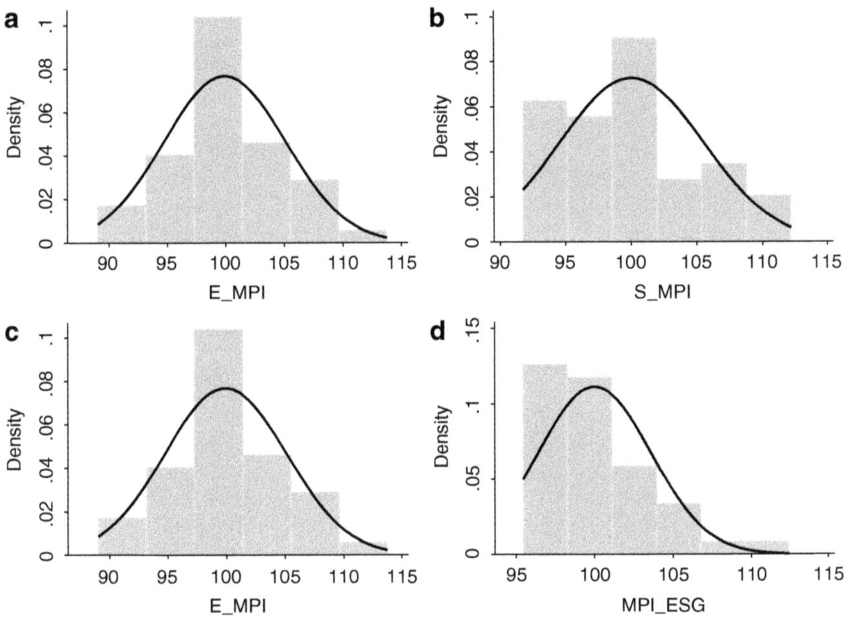

Fig. 4.2 MPI_ESG distribution—Breakdown by dimension and overall score. (a) Distribution of the MPI_E; (b) Distribution of the MPI_S, (c) Distribution of the MPI_G, (d) Distribution of the MPI_ESG. Source: Authors

observed in Social and Governance issues. However, additional efforts are required to align environmental performance with global objectives.

The resulting composite indicators for the E, S, and G dimensions, as well as the overall ESG composite indicator, are reported in Table 4.13, together with the corresponding enterprise rankings. To comply with data confidentiality commitments made to the respondents, enterprise

Table 4.13 Mazziotta–Pareto Index (MPI) scores by ESG dimension and overall ESG ranking

Enterprise	*E_MPI*	*S_MPI*	*G_MPI*	*MPI_ESG*	*Ranking*
1	108.0074	99.92451	94.0511	99.7791	18
2	97.8946	99.92451	96.7775	98.5744	26
3	98.8257	97.75957	100.6277	98.8332	22
4	98.6964	107.9168	103.7047	104.8091	3
5	102.8469	95.62573	103.7047	99.4936	19
6	98.8257	95.62573	103.5674	98.6482	24
7	98.8257	93.76337	103.7047	97.7582	29
8	94.7007	95.76382	102.0811	97.4464	32
9	94.7007	93.76337	101.1557	96.1686	36
10	99.4576	93.76337	97.5972	96.0524	39
11	94.7007	93.76337	99.9438	95.8050	40
12	98.8257	99.72613	103.7047	100.7396	13
13	99.4576	91.71672	101.1557	96.0966	38
14	98.8257	103.8324	99.9438	101.6645	10
15	98.8257	95.76382	96.2657	96.5268	34
16	98.6964	99.72613	96.6337	98.5925	25
17	102.8469	101.7896	100.5462	101.628	11
18	98.8257	97.68293	91.7349	96.1271	37
19	102.8469	93.76337	98.6684	97.0516	33
20	102.8469	102.0052	100.5462	101.7358	9
21	107.6548	99.72613	107.6415	103.6865	6
22	98.8257	93.76337	103.134	97.5870	30
23	98.8257	95.6257	103.7047	98.6894	23
24	98.8257	111.4609	90.4985	102.6452	8
25	98.8257	101.7896	85.4645	96.2993	35
26	108.9112	105.8545	103.7047	105.8209	2
27	102.8469	99.7261	98.7321	100.0521	17
28	103.6065	97.8917	94.7039	98.0783	27
29	94.7007	101.7896	97.2516	99.0104	20
30	98.8257	109.4299	97.2984	103.6696	7
31	89.0275	99.7117	99.5351	97.5219	31
32	107.6548	99.7913	96.7775	100.4598	16
33	104.7473	91.7167	103.7047	97.9192	28
34	94.7007	93.7634	98.7545	95.4482	41
35	89.0275	103.3082	98.3182	98.9551	21
36	97.1264	108.6509	102.4323	104.4804	4
37	108.9112	106.6305	96.7775	104.1307	5
38	98.6964	99.92451	102.5945	100.4799	15
39	93.1227	101.941	103.7047	100.7064	14
40	94.7007	105.1162	98.7321	101.1179	12
41	103.4871	108.0431	109.5557	107.5857	1

Source: Authors.

Table 4.14 Correlation matrix of the composite indicators vs global ESG CI

	G_MPI	*S_MPI*	*E_MPI*	*MPI_ESG*
G_MPI	1			
S_MPI	0.50761085	1		
E_MPI	0.05879153	0.05627367	1	
MPI_ESG	0.75046312	0.75678034	0.55291874	1

Source: Authors.

identities are anonymized and reported as Enterprises 1–41. Accordingly, the results reveal substantial heterogeneity in ESG performance across SMEs, both within and across dimensions. Several enterprises exhibit unbalanced ESG profiles, ranking highly in one pillar while performing relatively poorly in others.

The correlation matrix, present in Table 4.14, reveals that governance and social scores are moderately correlated (0.51), indicating that firms with stronger governance also tend to perform better on social aspects. Both dimensions are strongly associated with the global ESG score (0.75 and 0.76, respectively), making them the primary drivers of overall performance. By contrast, the environmental dimension appears largely independent from governance and social (correlations close to zero), yet still contributes moderately to the global score (0.55). This suggests that, within the sample, environmental practices are relatively decoupled from governance and social strategies, highlighting an asymmetry in the interaction between the three ESG pillars.

4.5 Conclusion

This chapter presents an approach of ESG composite index specifically designed for SMEs, providing a clearer understanding of the ESG performance of both small and medium-sized companies. In conclusion, our analysis reveals variations in ESG performance among the companies in our sample. We find that a company's poor performance in a single E, S, or G pillar may offset its strong performance in other pillars and even reduce its overall ESG ranking. To improve overall ESG performance, companies need to enhance at first E performance and better consolidate the S and G performance simultaneously.

Our study has several limitations. Firstly, our sample comprises only 42 companies from a limited number of sectors. This small sample size may limit to apply some additional robustness checks in our research estimations. In the future, we plan to reach out to a more diverse range of companies. Second, our analysis focuses on french firms in the Haut-de-France region. It could be interesting to expand the geographic scope to other regions or countries.

References

Agnese, P., Carè, R., Cerciello, M., & Taddeo, S. (2025). Reconsidering the impact of environmental, social and governance practices on firm profitability. *Management Decision*, *63*(1), 25–48.

Aouadi, A., & Marsat, S. (2018). Do ESG controversies matter for firm value? Evidence from international data. *Journal of Business Ethics*, *151*(4), 1027–1047.

Berg, F., Kölbel, J. F., & Rigobon, R. (2022). Aggregate confusion: The divergence of ESG ratings. *Review of Finance*, *26*(6), 1315–1344.

Bloomberg. (2025). Bloomberg ESG scores. https://professional.bloomberg.com/globalassets/professional/solutions/sustainable-finance/scores/bloombergesg-scores-methodology.pdf

Cerciello, M., Busato, F., & Taddeo, S. (2023). The effect of sustainable business practices on profitability: Accounting for strategic disclosure. *Corporate Social Responsibility and Environmental Management*, *30*(2), 802–819.

Chatterji, A. K., Durand, R., Levine, D. I., & Touboul, S. (2016). Do ratings of firms converge? Implications for managers, investors and strategy researchers. *Strategic Management Journal*, *37*(8), 1597–1614.

Christensen, D. M., Serafeim, G., & Sikochi, A. (2022). Why is corporate virtue in the eye of the beholder? The case of ESG ratings. *The Accounting Review*, *97*(1), 147–175.

De Muro, P., Mazziotta, M., & Pareto, A. (2011). Composite indices of development and poverty: An application to MDGs. *Social Indicators Research*, *104*(1), 1–18.

Dimson, E., Marsh, P., & Staunton, M. (2020). Divergent ESG ratings. London Business School.

Dorfleitner, G., Halbritter, G., & Nguyen, M. (2015). Measuring the level and risk of corporate responsibility: An empirical comparison of different ESG rating approaches. *Journal of Asset Management*, *16*(7), 450–466.

Dumrose, M., Rink, S., & Eckert, J. (2022). Disaggregating confusion? The EU taxonomy and its relation to ESG ratings. *Finance Research Letters*, *48*, 102928.

Escrig-Olmedo, E., Fernández-Izquierdo, M. Á., Ferrero-Ferrero, I., Rivera-Lirio, J. M., & Muñoz-Torres, M. J. (2019). Rating the raters: Evaluating how ESG rating agencies integrate sustainability principles. *Sustainability*, *11*(3), 915.

Gibson Brandon, R., Krueger, P., & Schmidt, P. S. (2021). ESG rating disagreement and stock returns. *Financial Analysts Journal*, *77*(4), 104–127.

ISS ESG. (2023). ESG corporate rating: Methodology and research process. https://www.issgovernance.com/file/products/iss-esg-corporate-rating-methodology.pdf

ISS ESG. (2024). ESG corporate rating survey. https://www.issgovernance.com/file/publications/iss-esg-corporate-rating-survey-summary-2024.pdf

London Stock Exchange Group (LSEG). (2024). Environmental, social and governance scores from LSEG: Methodology. https://www.lseg.com/content/dam/data-analytics/en_us/documents/methodology/lseg-esg-scores-methodology.pdf

Mazziotta, M., & Pareto, A. (2012). A non-compensatory approach for the measurement of the quality of life. In Maggino, F., & Nuvolati, G. (Eds.), *Quality of life in Italy: Research and reflections* (pp. 27–40). Springer. https://doi.org/10.1007/978-94-007-3898-0_3

Mazziotta, M., & Pareto, A. (2013). Methods for constructing composite indices: One for all or all for one? Rivista Italiana di Economia, *Demografia e Statistica*, *67*(2), 67–80.

Mazziotta, M., & Pareto, A. (2022). Weighting in composite indices construction: The case of the Mazziotta-Pareto index. Rivista Italiana di Economia, *Demografia e Statistica*, *76*(1), 17–26.

Morningstar Sustainalytics. (2024). The ESG risk ratings methodology. https://connect.sustainalytics.com/hubfs/INV/Methodology/Sustainalytics_ESG%20Ratings_Methodology%20Abstract.pdf

MSCI. (2025). ESG ratings: Assessing companies on financially relevant sustainability risks and opportunities. Retrieved July 10, 2025, from https://www.msci.com/data-and-analytics/sustainability-solutions/esg-ratings

OECD. (2008). *Handbook on constructing composite indicators: Methodology and user guide*. OECD Publishing.

Principles for Responsible Investment. (2025). PRI signatory directory. Retrieved July 10, 2025, from https://www.unpri.org/signatories/signatory-resources/signatory-directory

Refinitiv. (2022). Environmental, social and governance (ESG) scores from Refinitiv: Methodology. https://www.lseg.com/content/dam/marketing/en_us/documents/methodology/refinitiv-esg-scores-methodology.pdf

Annexes

Annex 4.1 Agency

Agency	*Bloomberg*	*MSCI*	*Sustainability*	*LSEG (Refinitiv)*	*ISS ESG Corporate Rating*
Measurement	Financially material ESG issues.	ESG risk exposure, and management of ESG risks and opportunities.	Sustainability risks linked with Material ESG Issues and Unmanaged Risk.	Companies' ESG performance, commitment, effectiveness, using data reported by the company.	Companies' ability to manage ESG risks, minimize impacts, create positive outcomes, and capitalize on sustainable development opportunities.
Scores Measurement	Best in class performance within peer groups. The scores are based on publicly available, company disclosed data, and do not rely on estimates or an analyst's opinion.	MSCI ESG rating assess companies by evaluating their exposure to and management of ESG risks and opportunities, using three pillars (E, S and G), in order to identify industry leaders and laggards based on their relative performance among peers.	The quantitative score presents risk categories (negligible, low, medium, high, severe), which indicate the level of unmanaged ESG risk, with lower scores signifying less unmanaged risk.	Over 630 ESG measures, with 186 key industry-specific measures used for scoring, focusing on ten categories of three pillars: E, S and G. Weights for the E and S pillars vary by industry, while G weights remain consistent.	A fixed twelve-point letter grading system with a corresponding numerical scale, incorporating weighting scenarios specific to industry rating structures.
Score range	0–10	AAA–CCC	0–50	From D- to A+	From D- (1) to A+ (4)
Best score	10	AAA	0–10 (negligible risk)	A+	A+ (4)
Overall ESG Score	Pillar weighting depends on the financial materiality of each pillar.	Assign percentage weights to each ESG risk, then combine and normalize the scores relative to industry peers to determine the overall ESG rating.	(1) 22 Material ESG Issues, (2) Corporate Governance & Stakeholder Governance, and (3) Systemic ESG Issues & Idiosyncratic Issues.	(1) ESG score, and (2) ESG controversies	(1) the Social and Governance Rating, and (2) the Environmental Rating

E pillar	Issue priorities: probability, magnitude and timing of impact.	Four themes and 13 key issues: climate change, natural capital, pollution & waste, environment opportunities.	Emissions, Effluents and Waste, Carbon—Own Operations or Productions and Services, E&S Impact of Products and Services, Land Use and Biodiversity, Raw Material Use, Water Use—Own Operations or Supply Chain.	68 metrics—Resource use—Emissions—Innovation.	Environmental Management Products and Services Environmental Impact of Products and Services Products Environmental Aspects along the Value Chain Eco-Efficiency.
S pillar	Issue priorities: probability, magnitude and timing of impact.	4 themes and 14 key issues—Human Capital—Product Liability—Stakeholder Opposition—Social Opportunities.	Access to Basic Services, Business Ethics, Community Relations, Data Privacy and Cybersecurity, E&S Impact of Products and Services, Human Rights, Human Capital, Occupational Health and Safety.	62 metrics—Workforce - Human rights—Community—Product responsibility.	Staff and Suppliers Society and Product Responsibility Corporate Governance and Business Ethics.
G pillar	Board Composition, Executive Compensation, Shareholder Rights and Audit.	2 themes and 6 key issues—Corporate Governance—Corporate Behavior.	Corporate Governance Stakeholder Governance Product Governance Resilience.	56 metrics—Management—Shareholders—CSR strategy.	Corporate Governance and Business Ethics.

Source: Authors.

Annex 4.2 Methodology of the Composite Indicator Creation

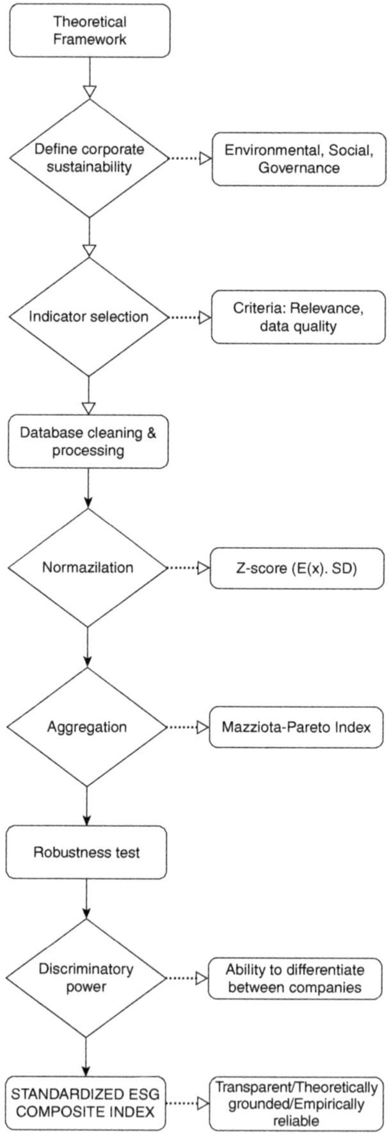

Source: Authors

CHAPTER 5

ESG Criteria Integration into Sustainable Business Models

Sandra Ramos, Fatma Güneri, and Hélène Ostrowski

Abstract This chapter examines the integration of Environmental, Social, and Governance (ESG) dimensions into Small and Medium-sized Enterprises (SMEs) business models. Zaman et al. (2025) highlighted that sustainability remains a multifaceted and evolving paradigm within economics and business. Small and medium-sized enterprises (SMEs) are crucial to the global economy, serving as essential threads in its fabric by driving innovation, creating jobs, and fostering resilience. Micro-enterprises alone represent between 70% and 90% of all firms in OECD countries (OECD, 2017), while SMEs contribute approximately 60% of total employment and value-added across these economies (OECD, 2017).

To integrate ESG criteria into business models, SMEs must depart from the traditional emphasis on financial performance alone. This requires an expanded conception of value creation that prioritizes environmental,

S. Ramos (✉) • F. Güneri
ICL, Junia, Université Catholique de Lille, LITL
e-mail: Sandra.RAMOS@univ-catholille.fr

H. Ostrowski
Autonomie et Solidarité (A&S), Lille, France

S. Kendo (ed.), *Non-Financial Reporting and ESG Performance*, Palgrave Studies in Impact Finance,
https://doi.org/10.1007/978-3-032-19092-5_5

social, and human capital stewardship and regeneration. This transition may involve either reconfiguring existing business models or designing entirely new sustainability-oriented frameworks.

The chapter is structured into two main sections. The first provides a literature review, synthesizing theoretical perspectives and empirical findings on the drivers, constraints, and strategic implications of ESG integration in SME contexts. It discusses resource limitations, regulatory asymmetries, and the lack of standardized ESG tools tailored to smaller firms. The second section presents a comparative analysis of three enterprises from the Autonomie & Solidarité portfolio (Bon Spot, CRESMAR, and IoT), illustrating diverse pathways of ESG integration. Through these case studies, the chapter highlights the operational challenges and the transformative potential of sustainability-aligned business models for SMEs.

Keywords ESG • Sustainable Business Model • SMEs • Drivers

5.1 Introduction

Sustainability, at the organizational level, refers to the integration of practices that balance economic growth with environmental and social responsibility, ensuring long-term success and positive contributions to society. Sustainability has become a vital component of organizations' strategies (Alsayegh et al., 2020). This concept has, therefore, redefined the parameters of corporate performance and value creation of all organizations, including SMEs. Regardless of their *liability of smallness* (Aldrich & Auster, 1986), SMEs (Small, and Medium-sized Enterprises) represent the backbone of the global economy, accounting for approximately 60% of total employment and value-added across OECD (Organisation for Economic Co-operation and Development) economies. Similarly, micro-enterprises account for between 70% to 90% of all firms (OECD, 2017).

Evaluating corporate performance nowadays extends beyond traditional financial metrics to encompass sustainability principles, aiming at creating value for all stakeholders. ESG serves as a holistic framework, enabling organizations to integrate sustainability principles into their Business Models (BMs). This integration is done by systematically embedding environmental sustainability, social responsibility, and governance ethics. It has transitioned from a peripheral concern to a central, strategic, and comprehensive role in business operations (Cek & Eyupoglu, 2020; Li et al., 2018).

Regulatory advancements, such as the European Sustainability Reporting Standards (ESRS) and the establishment of the International Sustainability Standards Board (ISSB), indicate a growing institutionalization of sustainability. SMEs, along with other organizations, must therefore incorporate sustainability criteria into their strategic and operational activities (Prashar & Sunder M, 2020). Such requirements prompt SMEs to balance their resource constraints and a certain degree of informality with the growing demand for transparency and accountability. Moreover, embracing sustainable practices enables SMEs to enhance competitiveness, foster stakeholder collaborations, and contribute to the principles of sustainable development (Zaman et al., 2025).

Dedicated frameworks and guidelines at the institutional level must be in place to guide SMEs in implementing sustainable practices. However, policymakers must consider the distinct characteristics of SMEs compared to larger corporations. Criteria suitable for large corporations may not be the best fit for SMEs. Notwithstanding this, various challenges persist in the adoption of sustainability frameworks by SMEs, including limited institutional support and insufficient recognition of the business benefits of sustainable principles (Martins et al., 2022).

It has been demonstrated (cf. Chap. 2) that organizations, regardless of their size, face increasing pressure from financial stakeholders, such as shareholders and investors, to adopt ESG criteria. Indeed, these stakeholders, keen to limit long-term risks, now demand detailed information on the environmental and social risks associated with their portfolios. Their new investment practices are to comply with strict EU (European Union) standards (Green Taxonomy and Sustainable Finance Disclosure Regulation).

This chapter aims to understand how micro-enterprises and SMEs integrate ESGs into their existing Business Models. The first section examines the recent literature review on the topics of Sustainable Business Models, ESG integration, and the drivers and challenges explicitly faced by SMEs. The empirical part focuses on three local SMEs, which make a concerted effort to integrate activities aligned with sustainable principles into their strategic and operational frameworks. Yet, they still face challenges, including the lack of institutional support and insufficient client interest in sustainable practices.

5.2 Literature Review

5.2.1 Conceptualizing Sustainable Business Models

Today's society is concerned with sustainability in business practices, encouraging organizations to embed sustainability criteria into their BMs (Bocken et al., 2014). BMs play a crucial role in enabling organizations to create and capture value (Ilyas & Osiyevskyy, 2022). Although the concept of BMs is viewed differently by various scholars, most conceptualizations at a broader level suggest three main elements: value proposition, value creation and delivery, and value capture. It is, ergo, a conceptual tool that describes how an organization does business and converts resources and capabilities into economic value (Teece, 2010). It is also defined as the "*value logic of an organization in terms of how it creates and captures customer value, representing the interrelated set of elements that address the customer, value proposition, organizational architecture, and economics dimensions.*" (Fielt, 2013, p. 86).

A Sustainable Business Model (SBM), also referred to as Business Models for Sustainability (Lüdeke-Freund, 2009). It follows the same logic as traditional BMs but also aims to address environmental and social challenges through the value-creating activities of the organization (Schaltegger et al., 2016). An organization operating an SBM would regenerate the ecological ecosystem, create value for stakeholders and society, and make a profit through its products and services. Lüdeke-Freund (2010) underlines that a business generating a competitive advantage by delivering superior customer value while contributing to sustainable development can be considered an SBM. Initial research on SBM is often rooted in environmental sustainability; however, some scholars also view it as a means to address social issues. The work of Seelos and Mair (2007) illustrates this direction.

The three elements of traditional and SBMs:

- Value proposition reflects the organization's offering to customers, serving as a strategic guide in both the creation and capture of value.
- Value creation and value delivery are closely tied to the organization's resources, capabilities, and inter-organizational components, including supply chain operations, organizational systems, and communication.
- Value capture is related to the cost structure and revenue model.

5.2.2 *ESG Integration into Business Models*

ESG refers to the Environmental, Social, and Governance criteria used by organizations and investors to assess corporate sustainability and ethical performance (Arora & Sharma, 2022). It provides, therefore, a holistic framework for monitoring and controlling the impact of the organization's practices both internally and externally. It goes beyond the economic and financial aspects (Cek & Eyupoglu, 2020). Through ESG criteria, organizations can provide both qualitative and quantitative information about sustainability practices to all stakeholders (Khalil et al., 2024; Uyar et al., 2023).

Corporate sustainability, through the integration of ESG criteria into BMs, serves as a tool used by organizations to integrate sustainability considerations into their business strategies, decision-making processes, and operational routines (Aldowaish et al., 2022). It is an organizational tool used to define, plan, operationalize, and execute actions directed at fulfilling sustainable practices (de Souza Barbosa et al., 2023).

Effectively, incorporating ESG criteria into organizational operations involves striking a balance between sustainability and economic, environmental, and social considerations while addressing operational, managerial, governance, and communication systems. It goes beyond mere compliance with regulations, as it involves embedding sustainability principles into the core business operations.

This transformation into SBMs and ESG integration is a response to normative and regulatory pressures at the sector, industry, and societal levels. It means that today, a multitude of stakeholders expect new models of production and consumption that align with sustainability principles (Nishitani et al., 2021). Over time, organizations have shifted from prioritizing shareholders' expectations exclusively to embracing the interests of a broader range of stakeholders. SBM engages a variety of stakeholders in management, innovation, and a long-term perspective to reduce the negative externalities on the environment and society, and thereby meeting sustainable goals (Nosratabadi et al., 2019).

5.2.3 *Drivers of ESG Integration in SMEs*

Few studies have examined the drivers of integrating ESG in SMEs' BMs and strategies. External and internal drivers influence organizations to adopt sustainability practices, but these practices can differ for SMEs. Yadav et al. (2018) indicate that external drivers, such as government regulation, legislation, and economic and structural support, are critical in influencing SMEs to adopt sustainable practices. Stakeholders, including government, customers, alliances, competitors, suppliers, and the community, can affect SMEs' behavior towards sustainability practices.

However, SMEs also have unique internal drivers of sustainability practices, such as independent ownership, which relies on reputation, agility, personal relationships, and informality, resulting in these smaller firms gaining a competitive advantage over larger organizations (Tsvetkova et al., 2020). Hence, adopting sustainability practices must be closely aligned with their unique internal drivers and business objectives.

5.2.4 *Challenges and Barriers to ESG Integration*

Although incorporating ESG practices into BMs has become essential and widely embraced, the process remains rather challenging due to both organizational and contextual barriers. Several studies have investigated barriers to corporate sustainability and ESG integration (Bebic et al., 2025; Mutua et al., 2025), as discussed in the following subsection.

At the organizational level, the literature highlights the limited financial resources available for investing in both organizational structures, tools, and human capital. Mutua et al. (2025) refers to the fact that integrating ESG requires additional costs for organizations, including data systems, hiring skilled employees, and compliance costs. Yet, failing to balance profit and sustainability risks widens the financial gap. Regarding human capital, authors highlight the lack of skills, expertise, and experience among the organization's employees, mainly regarding sustainability issues (Bebic et al., 2025).

In addition to the above, several other internal issues remain significant. The high complexity of existing sustainability management standards and tools often exceeds the absorptive capacity of SMEs (Schaltegger et al., 2016). The lack of awareness regarding the sustainability imperative, its advantages, and disadvantages (Díaz Díaz & García Ramos, 2015; Schaltegger et al., 2016). This negatively impacts the integration and reporting on ESG. Furthermore, Bebic et al. (2025) underscore internal conceptual ambiguity among employees as a critical challenge to effective

ESG integration. Organizations still face a low level of formalization of corporate sustainability, resulting in the absence of a dedicated organizational unit responsible for ESG strategies and actions (Beckers et al., 2013).

Externally, authors mention various barriers, all of which are interlinked with the lack of institutional support. Limited regulatory frameworks, characterized by non-inclusive and non-standardized guidelines, and the absence of supportive policy frameworks, are frequently mentioned in the literature (Bebic et al., 2025; Dos Santos et al., 2022; Lisi et al., 2024). SMEs, in particular, do not enjoy a tailored instrument explicitly designed according to their needs and characteristics (Schaltegger et al., 2016).

Bebic et al. (2025) also refer specifically to the complexity of the legal landscape. A panoply of terms and abbreviations exists that can create confusion among managers and employees alike. The fast-evolving legal and regulatory landscape of sustainable practices also creates a barrier for organizations that lack the necessary dynamic capacities. Regulatory gaps persist, creating additional challenges for organizations.

5.3 Case Studies

This study analyzes three SMEs located in the Hauts-de-France region, an industrial area undergoing transition, where economic, social, and environmental issues are particularly significant. These organizations stand out for the diversity of their business sectors, illustrating the cross-cutting nature of the challenges associated with integrating ESG criteria into their BMs (Table 5.1).

By the very nature of their activities, these three organizations provide a representative overview of the opportunities and challenges faced by SMEs in implementing an ESG approach. Their trajectories enable the identification of levers for action, as well as the recognition of structural tensions.

5.3.1 Presentation of the Three Organizations

5.3.2 ESG Criteria Integrated into the Business Model of the Three Organizations

In Table 5.2, the ESG-related practices of BON SPOT, CRESMAR, and IOT SYMPHONY are described.

Table 5.1 Presentation of the Business Models of the three organizations

BON SPOT	*CRESMAR*	*IOT SYMPHONY*
Value proposition: a variety of high-quality services—climbing gym, wellness centre, and restaurant—addressing issues of proximity, social ties, and responsible consumption.	*Value proposition:* provides high-quality, customizable floral products that accommodate their clients' needs, from everyday purchases to special events.	*Value proposition:* designs and distributes connected objects that are innovative, reliable, and tailored to meet the needs of modern users.
Value creation: • Large bouldering room, featuring 36 wall profiles and over 150 boulders. • Wellness center featuring a sauna and gym. • Restaurant open to all public. • Other amenities: society games and co-working spaces. Expert staff, route-setters, and instructors contribute to the well-curated client experience during their stay in the facility.	*Value creation:* • Products: fresh and artificial flowers, floral arrangements, and decorative items, all crafted by skilled florists who ensure quality and customization. • Services: self-service flowers, same-day delivery, parcel collection, flower subscriptions, online sales of bouquets and plants, and personalized advice. It nurtures brand loyalty by maintaining consistent quality, providing personalized customer service, and fostering a strong community presence, thereby ensuring sustained profitability and retaining customers.	*Value creation:* • Development and manufacture of innovative, high-quality electronic products. It aims to help companies maximize the benefits of audio IoT to enhance communication, efficiency, and user experience. • User-friendly software products – allowing expert-users to set up, manage, and monitor IoT audio environments from a single interface. • Sophisticated analytics tools provide detailed insights to optimize the operation of connected audio devices. • It is both a producer and wholesaler, which allows it to oversee the entire product lifecycle, from design to delivery.
Value delivery: Large, easily accessible, all-in-one facility.	*Value delivery:* network of physical retail locations across Hauts-de-France; e-commerce platform; Distribution services.	*Value delivery:* Wholesale and retail distribution approach (B2B and B2C).
Value capture: various channels: day passes, memberships, and fees from group events; additional revenues from restaurant, wellness area, equipment rental, and merchandise sales.	*Value capture:* through sales of its products and services (in-store and online channels).	*Value captures:* Sales of electronic products.

Source: Authors.

Table 5.2 ESG criteria integration into Business Models

Criteria	*BON SPOT*	*CRESMAR*	*IOT SYMPHONY*
Environmental	• Waste reduction, processing, and reuse. • Resoling and recycling climbing shoes. • Retexturing climbing holds. • Collaborations with a local business (for waste processing). • Partnerships with local suppliers for food, beverages, and wood.	• Waste management, water conservation, and energy efficiency. • Rainwater recovery. • Craft and recyclable materials (estimated 80% recyclable packaging usage). • Energy efficiency (LED lighting, motion sensors, and a single cold room). • Prioritization of electric vehicles and collaboration with partners that employ electric vehicles for deliveries. • Optimization of delivery logistics by combining orders wherever possible.	• Waste management and product eco-conception. • It strives to produce locally, at least within Europe (resulting in higher costs). • Attempts to use reusable packaging and consolidate parcels at collection points to minimize the number of trips. • It aims to tackle planned obsolescence by repairing its products whenever possible.
Social	• The team is mainly composed of young employees. • Social and economic committee to support employees' well-being and encourage dialogue in the workplace. • Provides training. • Set organizational goals. • Establishment of collective and individual bonuses based on performance.	• Adheres to the collective agreement established for its sector, ensuring compliance with industry standards. • Commits to continuously improving working conditions. Example: automated specific tasks to reduce physical strain and offered retraining opportunities for employees affected by occupational illnesses. • Automation of HR processes to enhance efficiency. • Recruitment is often conducted through apprenticeship programs, providing opportunities for successful candidates to secure permanent contracts and advance their careers.	• Operates on a collaborative principle. • Provides training to its employees to help them develop their skills and grow professionally. • The organization comprises a stable team of young professionals and experienced experts.

(continued)

Table 5.2 (continued)

Criteria	*BON SPOT*	*CRESMAR*	*IOT SYMPHONY*
Governance	• Governed by one director. • Decentralized approach, working closely with the teams on the ground. • Employees can participate in managerial decision-making.	• Hierarchical organizational structure, where managers oversee and guide staff. • Primarily managed by its founder (with > 20 years of experience). • Places high value on transparency and accountability.	• Two founders are actively involved. • Contribution of nine shareholders. • The long-term goal of the founders is to redistribute the value they create.

Source: Authors.

5.3.3 Drivers for ESG Incorporation into Business Models

Analysis of the three cases studied reveals that the integration of ESG criteria in SMEs is primarily driven by the potential to add value. It is the personal sensitivity and values of the manager/founder that drive the implementation of an ESG strategy, which in turn influences the value proposition. Leadership is, therefore, a key lever for initiating the transformation of BMs. Only BON SPOT has an employee who dedicates half a day per week to sustainability actions.

Another driver for implementing ESG practices is economic interest. This is key, as ESG is fully integrated when it generates concrete benefits for value creation (cost reduction, value chain optimization) and value delivery (customer loyalty through a consistent and responsible offering). Additionally, regulation acts as a framework for legitimacy. While not the primary factor, it remains crucial to gain credibility and capture value, thereby ensuring recognition and the long-term viability of the efforts made.

5.3.4 Does Integrating ESG into Business Models Generate Value?

In terms of the environment, the commitment of the three organizations is reflected in tangible operational practices. For example, BON SPOT focuses on waste reduction, reuse, and short supply chains, CRESMAR invests in water conservation and energy efficiency, and IOT SYMPHONY promotes eco-design and the repairability of its products. Simple, low-cost, and eco-friendly actions (such as waste management, soft mobility, and reduced consumption) can be easily adopted daily, generating immediate economic benefits.

On the social front, these organizations invest in training, ensure transparency in their interactions, and strengthen employee participation. For example, BON SPOT has an economic and social committee, CRESMAR has a hierarchical management structure with planned meetings, and IOT SYMPHONY has opted for collaborative decision-making processes. Employee involvement and hands-on management consolidate both value creation and delivery.

In terms of governance, the organizational structure of these organizations is centered around the leader(s)/entrepreneur(s). In addition, a lack of human and financial resources, as well as the absence of separation between decision-making and control powers, limit their room for maneuvering. However, each company is integrating initiatives to strengthen its governance, notably at IOT SYMPHONY with the establishment of a collaborative board with nine shareholders and at BON SPOT with its decentralized management structure.

Beyond its internal impact, ESG is also becoming a strategic differentiator, enabling organizations to build trust-based relationships with suppliers and customers who share the same values. This climate of cooperation fosters more sustainable value creation and capture, grounded in consistency, collective commitment, and the capacity for responsible innovation.

Furthermore, these organizations are part of a dynamic ecosystem. They are adapting their BMs to environmental and social trends to strengthen their value proposition and attractiveness to ESG-conscious stakeholders. At BON SPOT, for instance, this integration enhances the value captured, as investors and customers seek clear ethical commitments, which enable the company to gain market share in a competitive environment.

5.3.5 *Challenges in Integrating ESG into Business Models*

The three organizations studied have frequently encountered challenges when integrating ESG criteria into their BMs. While there is a genuine desire to commit, several internal and external barriers limit the scope of such efforts.

From an economic perspective, viability remains an essential requirement. ESG actions are prioritized when they generate a tangible return on investment. This logic of profitability sometimes limits the scope or sustainability of initiatives. For instance, IOT SYMPHONY relies on components primarily produced in China at more attractive costs.

Organizations have outlined challenges related to the supply chain. Sustainable local suppliers are hard to find, particularly for CRESMAR and IOT SYMPHONY, due to the sector in which they operate. These organizations struggle to structure their network of committed local suppliers. CRESMAR can only source its supplies in the Netherlands due to the volume and cost requirements. BON SPOT, meanwhile, sources its catering locally. As a result, organizations often compromise on the sustainability criteria to continue operating.

On the customer side, commitments vary. BON SPOT, on the one hand, reports that only some of its customers are willing to pay more to support local or sustainable practices. CRESMAR and IOT SYMPHONY, on the other hand, emphasize that their customers do not systematically consider ESG criteria as a purchasing criterion, particularly due to the more attractive prices of imported products. To remain competitive, organizations are forced to balance the integration of sustainability into their BMs.

Certain human and organizational constraints also weigh on the implementation of ESG actions. The restaurant industry, for BON SPOT, and the florist industry, for CRESMAR, are characterized by high turnover, low margins, and demanding work conditions. This limits staff investment in ESG initiatives, which are often perceived as additional work, and offers little flexibility to management.

Finally, the institutional and regulatory environment is considered unfavorable. The three organizations complain of a lack of support, concrete incentives, and adequate controls. For instance, BON SPOT is seeking to reduce waste but is unable to implement the resole of climbing shoes due to a lack of solutions in the industry. The absence of structured public action creates a gap between political rhetoric and operational reality. CRESMAR also highlights a lack of consistency in the priorities of public authorities and consumers, which makes it challenging to make decisions in favor of sustainable development.

These obstacles highlight a significant risk: if not pursued rigorously over the long term, the implementation of good ESG practices can quickly lose its effectiveness or even cancel out the value creation initially achieved. One-off actions that are not integrated into the overall strategy may be perceived as mere *greenwashing/socialwashing* or fail to bring about any lasting change. This undermines stakeholder trust and can discourage teams, thereby reducing the benefits in terms of image, performance, and loyalty.

5.3.6 Approaches to Strengthen the Societal Influence of SMEs and Promote ESG Incorporation into Business Models

Based on the analysis above, these three organizations can be considered exemplary in terms of ESG practices. Nevertheless, each suffers from constraints related to its industry, competitive pressures in its market, and social and economic tensions. To strengthen and sustain their efforts, SMEs require significant human and financial resources. The following sub-section discusses recommendations at the organizational and institutional levels.

At the organizational level, leaders should seek specific support to implement their ESG strategy. This involves establishing methods and indicators that are consistent with their BM and sector of activity. In addition, effective management, leadership, and internal consistency are essential to firmly anchor the value chain in a virtuous ESG dynamic. The gradual expansion of an ESG strategy, which involves all stakeholders at every stage of value creation, is a key factor in achieving success.

Next, the sustainability of value creation depends on rigorous monitoring and constant communication. Systematically promoting ESG practices lends credibility to actions, providing clarity and enhancing trust among all stakeholders. This step reinforces the collective responsible dynamic and maximizes the impact of the ESG strategy, ensuring its long-term viability while preventing initiatives from becoming mere *greenwashing/socialwashing*.

SMEs are key drivers of change in their local areas, capable of influencing the ecosystem. However, to maximize this societal influence, public authorities must support them. At the institutional level, public actors are the most potent vehicle for influence when it comes to implementing systemic action. The mobilization of professional federations would enable the implementation of collective initiatives tailored to specific sectors. Similarly, support from local authorities would ensure that voluntary measures are not the only response. The stakes are high, since according to the European Commission's (2024) report on SMEs, they account for 99.8% of non-financial organizations in the European Union. They therefore play a crucial role in raising awareness of ESG issues.

5.3.6.1 SWOT and TWOS Analysis

Table 5.3 presents a brief SWOT (strengths, weaknesses, oportunities, and threats) analysis of the factors affecting the organizations studied in this chapter. The recommendations, framed through a TOWS (threats, opportunities, weaknesses, and strengths) matrix, are intended for both micro-enterprises and SMEs wishing to incorporate ESG criteria into their BMs, as well as for the supportive ecosystem, such as public authorities and federations.

5.4 Conclusion

This chapter concludes that SMEs are willing and committed to integrating ESG criteria into their BMs. It is often the CEO who provides the necessary impetus for the sustainability strategy, as the CSRD (Corporate Sustainability Reporting Directive) does not yet bind SMEs. The implementation of ESG criteria enhances the value proposition and value capture

Table 5.3 SWOT and TOWS analysis

		INTERNAL	
		FORCES • Personal conviction and commitment (leadership). • Implementation of eco-friendly actions. • Various benefits include energy savings, improved image, and enhanced supplier relations.	**WEAKNESSES** • Financial constraints: profitability remains a priority. • Lack of structured support. • Difficulty in structuring local value chains. • Professions or sectors under pressure. • Uneven employees buy-in. • The size of structures limits capacity for action and availability of resources.
EXTERNAL	**OPPORTUNITIES** • Stakeholder pressure on ESG issues and the need for transparency. • Existing labels for large companies. • Regulations in favor of ESG actions. **THREATS** • Growing environmental and social constraints. • Discrepancy exists between public discourse and the on-the-ground constraints. • Lack of coordination between the private sector, public institutions, and consumers. • Weak regulatory controls. • Heavy dependence on specific markets or suppliers. • Competition with non-ESG-driven companies with lower costs.	• Training in participatory management to improve internal buy-in. • Create simplified labels tailored to micro-enterprises and SMEs to gain customer trust. • Joint pooling resources (purchasing groups, local platforms). • Integrate ESG into the purpose of products. • Increase support from federations and local authorities. • Promote and recognize SMEs adopting ESG strategies.	• Development of sector-specific best practice guides and mobilization of national federations on ESG issues. • Promotion of social dialogue. • Financial and human support from public authorities to structure ESG initiatives. • Creation of ESG support centers for SMEs. • Promote cooperation between local actors and the creation of local value chains to limit dependence on international suppliers. • Enforce existing regulations with a clear system of incentives or disincentives.

Source: Authors.

in several key ways, including improved product quality, traceability of the value chain, and greater transparency.

Unfortunately, SMEs also face several economic (market, prices, etc.), social (employees, consumers, shareholders), and political (regulation, lack of government support) obstacles. Through the TOWS analysis, the study highlights several potential actions to support sustainable business practices, particularly by strengthening links between the public and private spheres. These actions also include strategic support and the adaptation of incentive policies.

Finally, this chapter shows us that sustainable ideals are confronted with the organizational and economic reality of businesses. This gap can be explained by the *triangle of inaction* (Gifford, 2011), in which managers are caught between strong economic expectations (profitability, short-termism), a certain institutional inertia (lack of concrete support or administrative simplification), and consumers who are not very aware, mobilized, or unwilling to support more sustainable products.

Given that organizations only produce in response to customer needs and within regulatory and market constraints, future research could benefit from shifting the analytical focus to the broad organizational ecosystem. Other stakeholders are equally responsible for leveraging sustainable development. Hence, an effective sustainability strategy may lie in the coordinated actions of a range of stakeholders, rather than in isolated organizational initiatives.

References

Aldowaish, A., Kokuryo, J., Almazyad, O., & Goi, H. C. (2022). Environmental, social, and governance integration into the business model: Literature review and research agenda. *Sustainability, 14*(5), 2959. https://doi.org/10.3390/su14052959

Aldrich, H. E., & Auster, E. R. (1986). Even dwarfs started small: Liabilities of age and size and their strategic implications. *Research in Organizational Behavior, 8*, 165–198.

Alsayegh, M. F., Rahman, R. A., & Homayoun, S. (2020). Corporate economic, environmental, and social sustainability performance transformation through ESG disclosure. *Sustainability, 12*(9), 3910. https://doi.org/10.3390/su12093910

Arora, A., & Sharma, D. (2022). Do environmental, social and governance (ESG) performance scores reduce the cost of debt? Evidence from Indian firms. *Australasian Accounting, Business and Finance Journal, 16*(5), 4–18. https://doi.org/10.14453/aabfj.v16i5.02

Bebic, M., Badie, N. B., Tyll, L., & Srivastava, M. (2025). Exploring the barriers and drivers of ESG in the German Mittelstand: A qualitative analysis of mechanical and plant engineering companies. *Corporate Social Responsibility and Environmental Management, 32*(2), 2147–2170. https://doi.org/10.1002/csr.3054

Beckers, C., Marz, O., & Kolbe, L. M. (2013). Investing in sustainability: A practice-oriented approach to analyze IT-investments in sustainability reporting systems. *International Journal of Social Ecology and Sustainable Development, 4*(2), 99–120. https://doi.org/10.4018/jsesd.2013040106

Bocken, N. M. P., Short, S. W., Rana, P., & Evans, S. (2014). A literature and practice review to develop sustainable business model archetypes. *Journal of Cleaner Production, 65*, 42–56. https://doi.org/10.1016/j.jclepro.2013.11.039

Cek, K., & Eyupoglu, S. (2020). Does environmental, social and governance performance influence economic performance? *Journal of Business Economics and Management, 21*(4), 1165–1184. https://doi.org/10.3846/jbem.2020.12725

de Souza Barbosa, A., da Silva, M. C. B. C., da Silva, L. B., Morioka, S. N., & de Souza, V. F. (2023). Integration of environmental, social, and governance (ESG) criteria: Their impacts on corporate sustainability performance. *Humanities and Social Sciences Communications, 10*, 410. https://doi.org/10.1057/s41599-023-01919-0

Díaz Díaz, B., & García Ramos, R. (2015). Corporate social responsibility: Current and future perspectives in Spain. In S. O. Idowu, R. Schmidpeter, & M. S. Fifka (Eds.), *Corporate social responsibility in Europe* (pp. 413–433). Springer. https://doi.org/10.1007/978-3-319-13566-3_23

Dos Santos, P. G., Albuquerque, F., Rodrigues, M. A. B., & Morais, A. I. (2022). The views of stakeholders on mandatory or voluntary use of a simplified standard on non-financial information for SMEs in the European Union. *Sustainability, 14*(5), 2816. https://doi.org/10.3390/su14052816

European Commission. (2024). *Annual report on European SMEs 2023/2024*. Publications Office of the European Union.

Fielt, E. (2013). Conceptualising business models: Definitions, frameworks and classifications. *Journal of Business Models, 1*(1), 85–105.

Gifford, R. (2011). The dragons of inaction: Psychological barriers that limit climate change mitigation and adaptation. *American Psychologist, 66*(4), 290–302. https://doi.org/10.1037/a0023566

Ilyas, I. M., & Osiyevskyy, O. (2022). Exploring the impact of sustainable value proposition on firm performance. *European Management Journal, 40*(5), 729–740. https://doi.org/10.1016/j.emj.2021.09.009

Khalil, M. A., Khalil, R., & Khalil, M. K. (2024). Environmental, social and governance (ESG)-augmented investments in innovation and firms' value: A fixed-effects panel regression of Asian economies. *China Finance Review International, 14*(1), 76–102. https://doi.org/10.1108/cfri-05-2022-0067

Lisi, S., Mignacca, B., & Grimaldi, M. (2024). Non-financial reporting and SMEs: A systematic review, research agenda, and novel conceptualization. *Journal of Management & Organization, 30*(3), 600–622. https://doi.org/10.1017/jmo.2023.43

Li, Y., Gong, M., Zhang, X. Y., & Koh, L. (2018). The impact of environmental, social, and governance disclosure on firm value: The role of CEO power. *The British Accounting Review, 50*(1), 60–75. https://doi.org/10.1016/j.bar.2017.09.007

Lüdeke-Freund, F. (2009). Business model concepts in corporate sustainability contexts: From rhetoric to a generic template for business models for sustainability. *SSRN Electronic Journal.* https://doi.org/10.2139/ssrn.1544847

Lüdeke-Freund, F. (2010). Towards a conceptual framework of business models for sustainability. In *Knowledge collaboration & learning for sustainable innovation* (Conference proceedings of ERSCP & EMSU). https://doi.org/10.13140/RG.2.1.2565.0324

Martins, A., Branco, M. C., Melo, P. N., & Machado, C. (2022). Sustainability in small and medium-sized enterprises: A systematic literature review and future research agenda. *Sustainability, 14*(11), 6493. https://doi.org/10.3390/su14116493

Mutua, K., Powell-Turner, J., Spiers, M., & Callaghan, J. (2025). An in-depth analysis of barriers to corporate sustainability. *Administrative Sciences, 15*(5), 161. https://doi.org/10.3390/admsci15050161

Nishitani, K., Nguyen, T. B. H., Trinh, T. Q., Wu, Q., & Kokubu, K. (2021). Are corporate environmental activities to meet sustainable development goals (SDGs) simply greenwashing? An empirical study of environmental management control systems in Vietnamese companies from the stakeholder management perspective. *Journal of Environmental Management, 296*, 113364. https://doi.org/10.1016/j.jenvman.2021.113364

Nosratabadi, S., Mosavi, A., Shamshirband, S., Zavadskas, E. K., Rakotonirainy, A., & Chau, K. W. (2019). Sustainable business models: A review. *Sustainability, 11*(6), 1663. https://doi.org/10.3390/su11061663

OECD. (2017). *Small, medium, strong: Trends in SME performance and business conditions.* OECD Publishing. https://doi.org/10.1787/9789264275683-en

Prashar, A., & Sunder M, V. (2020). A bibliometric and content analysis of sustainable development in small and medium-sized enterprises. *Journal of Cleaner Production, 245*, 118665. https://doi.org/10.1016/j.jclepro.2019.118665

Schaltegger, S., Hansen, E. G., & Lüdeke-Freund, F. (2016). Business models for sustainability: Origins, present research, and future avenues. *Organization & Environment, 29*(1), 3–10. https://doi.org/10.1177/1086026615599806

Seelos, C., & Mair, J. (2007). Profitable business models and market creation in the context of deep poverty: A strategic view. *Academy of Management Perspectives, 21*(4), 49–63. https://doi.org/10.5465/amp.2007.27895339

Teece, D. J. (2010). Business models, business strategy and innovation. *Long Range Planning, 43*(2–3), 172–194. https://doi.org/10.1016/j.lrp.2009.07.003

Tsvetkova, D., Bengtsson, E., & Durst, S. (2020). Maintaining sustainable practices in SMEs: Insights from Sweden. *Sustainability, 12*(24), 10242. https://doi.org/10.3390/su122410242

Uyar, A., Kuzey, C., & Karaman, A. S. (2023). Does aggressive environmental, social, and governance engagement trigger firm risk? The moderating role of executive compensation. *Journal of Cleaner Production, 398*, 136542. https://doi.org/10.1016/j.jclepro.2023.136542

Yadav, N., Gupta, K., Rani, L., & Rawat, D. (2018). Drivers of sustainability practices and SMEs: A systematic literature review. *European Journal of Sustainable Development, 7*(4), 531–548. https://doi.org/10.14207/ejsd.2018.v7n4p531

Zaman, M., Tanewski, G., & Ekanayake, G. (2025). What does sustainability mean for small and medium enterprises: A systematic literature review. *Journal of Cleaner Production, 492*, 144830. https://doi.org/10.1016/j.jclepro.2025.144830

CHAPTER 6

Regulatory Framework: From Traditional Accounting to Non-Financial Accounting

Jean Daniel Wecxsteen, Sandra Kendo, Oussama Kacemi, and Safia Gherab

Abstract This chapter addresses the paradigm shift from traditional financial accounting to integrated reporting incorporating environmental, social, and governance (ESG) dimensions. In continuity with prior chapters, it focuses on how regulatory developments, particularly the EU's Corporate Sustainability Reporting Directive (CSRD) and European Sustainability Reporting Standards (ESRS), are transforming accounting practices, especially for SMEs.

The chapter is structured into three sections. The first traces the historical evolution of accounting standards, highlighting the growing importance of extra-financial information. It emphasizes the increasing influence of stakeholders and neo-institutional theories in expanding corporate responsibility frameworks.

The second section explores methodological approaches to integrated accounting. It presents the CARE method, which tackles green accounting

J. D. Wecxsteen • S. Kendo (✉) • O. Kacemi • S. Gherab
ICL, Junia, Université Catholique de Lille, LITL
e-mail: sandra.kendo@univ-catholille.fr

S. Kendo (ed.), *Non-Financial Reporting and ESG Performance*,
Palgrave Studies in Impact Finance,
https://doi.org/10.1007/978-3-032-19092-5_6

by treating natural and human capital as depreciable assets, and the SEMA approach, a participatory framework tailored for SMEs that prioritizes materiality and stakeholder engagement. Both methodologies address the inadequacy of traditional accounting systems in capturing sustainability-related impacts, offering proportionate and actionable solutions.

The third section presents a detailed case study: BON SPOT. This SME illustrates practical pathways for integrating ESG into business strategy, operations, and product innovation. Their experiences underscore key challenges—resource constraints, data complexity, and evolving standards—while demonstrating that phased, pragmatic sustainability implementation can yield competitive and relational advantages.

This chapter ultimately argues that integrating extra-financial reporting into SME accounting is not merely a regulatory obligation but a strategic opportunity to reshape value creation in the sustainability era.

Keywords Non-Financial Accounting • ESG • SMEs • Green Accounting

6.1 Introduction

The global business environment is experiencing a profound transformation driven by growing environmental concerns, social awareness, and governance expectations. Traditional financial reporting, while remaining fundamental, is increasingly viewed as insufficient to capture the full spectrum of an organization's performance and impact. This evolution reflects a deeper reconceptualization of business purpose and success metrics, challenging conventional accounting practices that have remained relatively unchanged for decades. For Small and Medium Enterprises (SMEs), this shift presents both unprecedented challenges and significant opportunities that require careful navigation.

SMEs today face a dual imperative: respond to market expectations for greater transparency around sustainability performance while adapting to an increasingly stringent regulatory environment. The European Union's Corporate Sustainability Reporting Directive (CSRD) and the emerging European Sustainability Reporting Standards (ESRS) signal a formalization of requirements previously considered voluntary. As large corporations implement these frameworks, they inevitably extend sustainability expectations throughout their supply chains, creating ripple effects that reach smaller businesses. Simultaneously, investors, customers, and employees increasingly factor environmental and social considerations into their decisions, creating market-driven incentives for sustainability integration. The distinctive characteristics of SMEs (limited financial resources, smaller teams with generalist rather than specialist roles, and often owner-centered decision-making) create unique challenges in adopting extra-financial reporting practices. Unlike larger organizations that can deploy dedicated sustainability departments, smaller enterprises must integrate these new requirements within existing operational structures. This resource reality necessitates adapted approaches that balance comprehensiveness with practicality, avoiding the simple downscaling of frameworks designed for multinational corporations.

While regulatory compliance often serves as the initial driver for sustainability reporting, forward-thinking SMEs recognize opportunities beyond mere conformity. Environmental and social performance metrics can inform strategic decision-making, operational improvements, and stakeholder communications. As demonstrated some companies like BON SPOT, sustainability integration can unlock differentiation advantages, strengthen stakeholder relationships, and drive innovation. The challenge lies in translating complex reporting frameworks into practical tools that enhance rather than burden business operations. The accounting profession itself is undergoing a significant transformation, with new methodologies emerging to capture previously externalized impacts. Approaches such as the CARE method (Comprehensive Accounting in Respect of Ecology) and SEMA (Socio-Economic and Multi-referential Accounting) represent attempts to integrate financial and non-financial dimensions within coherent frameworks. These developments challenge traditional accounting's focus on financial capital alone, expanding to include considerations of natural and human capital. For SMEs, this evolution requires not only new technical knowledge but also conceptual shifts in how business performance is understood and measured.

This chapter aims to provide actionable guidance for SMEs navigating the complex terrain of integrated reporting. For researchers, it offers a structured analysis of how extra-financial considerations intersect with traditional accounting in smaller organizations. For practitioners, it provides actionable insights and implementation strategies adaptable to resource-constrained environments. By bridging theoretical frameworks with practical applications, the chapter seeks to advance the conversation around proportionate, value-adding approaches to sustainability integration for SMEs. This chapter is organized into three complementary sections.

Section 1 examines the evolving regulatory landscape, tracing the development from traditional accounting standards to extra-financial reporting frameworks, with a particular focus on the implications for SMEs. Section 2 explores methodological approaches and practical tools for integrating financial and sustainability dimensions in smaller organizations. Section 3 presents detailed case study of one SME-BON SPOT—that have successfully implemented integrated approaches, highlighting both challenges encountered and strategies employed. Together, these sections provide a comprehensive overview of the theoretical foundations, practical considerations, and real-world applications of green accounting for SMEs.

6.2 The Development of Accounting Standards and Their Impact on SMEs

The globalization of economic exchanges has fundamentally transformed accounting practices over recent decades. As international transactions intensified, the need for a common financial language became imperative, leading to the development of International Financial Reporting Standards (IFRS). These standards, which replaced the International Accounting Standards (IAS) in 2005, represent more than just a terminological change—they mark a conceptual expansion from traditional "accounting" to "financial reporting" reflecting a more comprehensive approach to corporate communications.

Today, approximately 150 countries apply IFRS, with the European Union implementing them through Regulation (EC) No. 1606/2002. However, their application varies significantly for smaller entities. While Article 4 of this regulation requires listed companies to prepare consolidated financial statements in accordance with IFRS, Article 5 grants member states flexibility regarding non-listed companies, creating a variable regulatory landscape for SMEs.

For smaller enterprises, national frameworks retain considerable importance. In France, the "*Autorité des Normes Comptables (ANC)*" oversees a multi-tiered normative structure including the Plan Comptable Général and various sectoral standards. Created in 2009, the ANC not only establishes domestic rules but also participates in international standard-setting processes.

The International Accounting Standards Board attempted to address SME-specific concerns by developing IFRS for SMEs in 2009 (revised in 2015 and 2023). However, as Quagli and Paoloni (2012) observe: "*Simplified international standards often remain excessively complex for typical European SMEs.*" This assessment is shared by several European authorities, with France, Germany, and Italy advocating for more proportionate approaches.

Company Type	*Individual Accounts*	*Consolidated Accounts*
Listed Companies	French Norms.	IFRS Norms.
Non-Listed Companies	French Norms.	Optional IFRS Norms.

6.2.1 The Rise of Extra-Financial Considerations to Enrich ESG Accounting

Alongside accounting standardization, a profound transformation in business philosophy has been observed. The claim made in 1970 by Milton Friedman that "the social responsibility of business is to increase its profits" has gradually been challenged in favour of more inclusive perspectives. This evolution has been explained through two complementary theoretical frameworks. Within the Stakeholder Theory, proposed in 1984 by Edward Freeman, it has been argued that all actors interacting with a company should be considered in strategic decision-making, thereby extending corporate responsibility beyond shareholders to include employees, customers, suppliers, communities, and other stakeholders. Simultaneously, the Neo-Institutional Theory, developed in 1983 by DiMaggio and Powell, has demonstrated that organizational behavior is shaped by institutional and social contexts, often beyond the discretion of managers.

This conceptual evolution manifests in Environmental, Social, and Governance (ESG) criteria—a structured framework for evaluating corporate sustainability (Quairel, 2006). While Corporate Social Responsibility (CSR) describes a general approach to integrating social and environmental considerations, ESG provides specific metrics for investors assessing sustainability performance.

As BlackRock CEO Larry Fink stated in his influential 2020 letter to CEOs: "*I believe we are on the edge of a fundamental reshaping of finance ... Climate risk is investment risk.*" This perspective has gained significant traction, with ESG considerations now integral to investment decisions and increasingly important to employees seeking alignment with organizational values.

6.2.2 *The European Regulatory Response*

The European Union has progressively formalized sustainability reporting requirements. The Corporate Sustainability Reporting Directive (CSRD), succeeding the 2014 Non-Financial Reporting Directive (NFRD), significantly expands both the scope and depth of disclosure obligations.

The CSRD requires qualifying companies to "include sustainability information in their management report or publish a separate sustainability statement." Implementation follows a phased approach, beginning with financial institutions and large listed companies for the fiscal year 2024.

Companies exceeding two of three thresholds for two consecutive years fall under the directive:

- Average employees exceeding 250.
- Balance sheet total exceeding €25 million.
- Turnover exceeding €50 million.

The European Sustainability Reporting Standards (ESRS) underpin these disclosures, introducing the principle of "double materiality"—an innovative concept requiring companies to assess both:

- Sustainability risks affecting the company.
- The company's impact on society and the environment.

Double materiality represents a paradigm shift in corporate reporting by acknowledging the bidirectional relationship between business and society. This framework organizes disclosures across four domains: cross-cutting standards, environmental standards, social standards, and governance standards.

Critically for smaller enterprises, the CSRD creates ripple effects throughout supply chains. As the Barometer of Sustainability Reporting (2023) notes: "While SMEs may not meet direct reporting thresholds, 68% report receiving sustainability information requests from larger business partners." Fig. 6.1 provides a comprehensive overview of SME (Small, and Medium-sized Enterprises) engagement and its update process, highlighting the impact on business partners. This indirect effect stems from large companies' obligation to report on their entire value chain, inevitably drawing in smaller suppliers and partners.

The European Financial Reporting Advisory Group (EFRAG) plays a central role in shaping sustainability reporting standards in the European

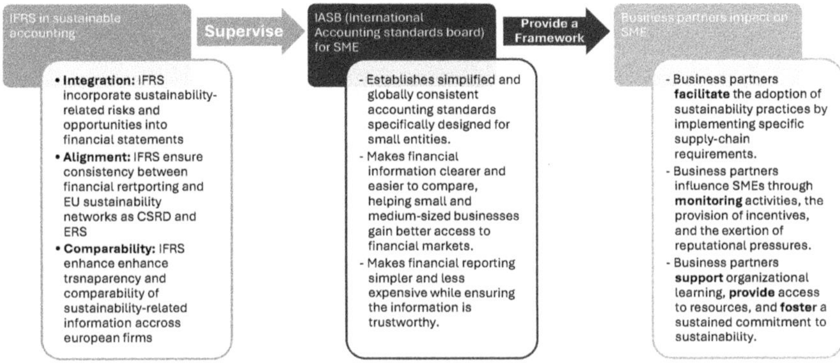

Fig. 6.1 Norms applications for SMEs. Source: Authors

Union. Established in 2001 as a non-profit association, EFRAG provides technical advice to the European Commission, particularly in the development and implementation of the European Sustainability Reporting Standards (ESRS). Its dual mission encompasses both the endorsement of International Financial Reporting Standards (IFRS) within the EU (European Union) and the advancement of corporate sustainability reporting practices. As part of the CSRD implementation, EFRAG is responsible for drafting the technical content of the ESRS, ensuring that the standards reflect the EU's policy objectives on sustainable finance and the principle of double materiality. The sustainability information disclosed under these standards must be verified by either a statutory auditor or an independent assurance services provider, thereby reinforcing the credibility and comparability of non-financial disclosures.

6.3 Green Accounting and ESG: Challenges and Opportunities for SMEs

6.3.1 The Need for Accounting Transformation

The limitations of traditional financial accounting have become increasingly apparent in today's sustainability-focused business environment. Conventional frameworks fail to capture critical dimensions of organizational performance, particularly environmental and social impacts. This narrow focus creates a distorted view of corporate value, where ecological degradation and social costs remain invisible in financial statements. For SMEs, this accounting gap presents both risks and opportunities. While they face pressure to adopt new reporting standards, they also stand to gain competitive advantages through the early adoption of integrated accounting practices.

The evolution toward green accounting reflects broader societal demands for corporate accountability (Rounaghi, 2019). Stakeholders ranging from investors to customers now expect businesses to demonstrate their sustainability performance with the same rigor as their financial results. This shift has been accelerated by regulatory developments, such as the EU's Corporate Sustainability Reporting Directive (CSRD), which introduces the principle of "double materiality" requiring companies to report both how sustainability issues affect their business and how their operations impact society and the environment.

6.3.2 Methodological Approaches to Integrated Accounting

6.3.2.1 The CARE Method: A Revolutionary Framework

The CARE method (Comprehensive Accounting in Respect of Ecology) is a conceptual framework and accounting methodology designed to reconceptualize the accounting of organizations (both private and public) on a fully ecological basis (ORSE, 2021). It seeks to place, at the heart of financial statements and performance analysis, the obligation to preserve "capital entities"—natural and human—employed by the organization, by establishing the principle that profit can only be calculated after guaranteeing the "repayment" of the ecological debt, in the same way that financial capital is preserved.

Developed since 2013 by a community of researchers, practitioners, businesses, and NGOs, the project is scientifically supported by the « Comptabilité Écologique » Chair (AgroParisTech, Paris-Dauphine University, University of Reims Champagne-Ardenne, Louis Bachelier Institute) and, on the practitioner/NGO side, by CERCES (cercle des comptables environnementaux et sociaux). It is the subject of numerous experiments (including those conducted by large companies, SMEs, and public organizations) and ongoing research programs. The founding texts and theoretical developments are notably associated with A. Rambaud and J. Richard (see Richard and Rambaud, 2018).

The method is part of a context of international race for "extra-financial" standardization and strong expectations regarding the consideration of socio-environmental issues. CARE stands out from several approaches to socio-environmental accounting that extend neoclassical logic (shareholder value, natural/human capital understood as productive assets, and internalization of externalities): these approaches, even when supplemented by pricing of externalities, do not guarantee ecosystem preservation. CARE, on the other hand, proposes a structural reorientation of accounting.

6.3.2.2 CARE's Central Ambition is Twofold

1. To reshape accounting so that it organizes the company's accountability for the natural and human capital it employs, ensuring its preservation;
2. To articulate non-financial, financial, and monetary information symmetrically, by assessing the real costs of preservation and integrating them into the accounts (balance sheet, income statement, appendices) and business models. CARE thus aims for strong sustainability, where each capital entity must be preserved individually.

CARE is not limited to a theoretical framework; it proposes a methodology (version V2) in eight phases that restructures dashboards, indicators, the business model, the chart of accounts, and financial documents (ORSE, 2021).

This approach combines biophysical and monetary accounting, connecting extra-financial considerations to financial accounting. Monetization is done at the expense of actual conservation activities, rather than through valuations based on the benefits provided by nature/humans (a logic rejected because it financializes nature and does not guarantee preservation).

Several challenges emerge from the project's experiments and literature. Firstly, the absence or heterogeneity of data (biophysical/monetary) sometimes requires recommendations and additional collection efforts, including by public authorities. Secondly, the reorganization of the chart of accounts and the creation of ecological liabilities require profound changes to systems. Thirdly, the definition of capital and its good condition requires a collective agreement (scientific and social) and inter-stakeholder dialogue when natural capital is shared. Lastly, CARE rejects monetization through benefits/"services" and promotes an assessment based on preservation costs, a condition for strong sustainability.

6.3.2.3 *The SeMA Approach: Stakeholder-Centric Accounting*

The SeMA (Sense-Making Accounting) method is part of the "integrated accounting" movement, which aims to intelligibly link an organization's financial accounts to its environmental and social impacts. The objective of SeMA is twofold: to make non-financial information operational for internal management and to create an accountability framework that informs governance decisions.

Historically, SeMA emerged in academic and professional networks as a means to seek pragmatic solutions that overcome the silos between financial reporting and ESG reporting. The method was designed as a practical response to the difficulties encountered by organizations, particularly SMEs, in linking their impacts to their accounts and budgetary decisions. It extends the work of integrated accounting while adopting a pragmatic stance: making existing accounts "talk" by adding an impact interpretation column, in a traceable and understandable manner for stakeholders. The purpose of SeMA is to objectify impacts and turn them into a genuine management signal. Concretely, the method aims to make non-financial arguments more reliable by explaining the assumptions, factors, and scopes used to link an impact to a given flow, and then bringing this information to the attention of decision-making bodies.

From a methodological perspective, SeMA favors a flow-based and impact-area approach. The most impactful accounting transactions (for example, certain purchasing or investment items) are identified and linked to relevant environmental and social indicators (air emissions, water consumption, potential impacts on biodiversity, social dimensions). Where relevant and feasible, simplified life cycle analyses can be used to prioritize actions. The results are then presented in the form of "augmented" financial statements, where the impact analysis complements the financial analysis to promote decision-making and managerial consistency.

The SeMA approach thus emphasizes intelligibility, traceability, and decision-making. Impact information is linked to identified lines of business, enabling a discussion of its relevance, scope, and underlying assumptions. This granularity facilitates dialogue between financial, CSR, and operational departments by bringing environmental and social issues back to the heart of budgetary and investment processes.

However, the implementation of SeMA faces several recurring challenges. Firstly, the availability and quality of data to link impacts to accounting flows (particularly for SMEs). Secondly, the choice of robust and transparent assumptions and assessment factors is critical when a simplified life cycle analysis is used. Thirdly, taking into account extended scopes (upstream/downstream value chain) and the allocation of responsibilities. Lastly, the legal and accounting constraints surrounding the translation of impacts into accounting entries (e.g., creation of provisions) require close dialogue with the financial department and auditors.

6.3.3 Outlook and Non-Financial Accounting Perspectives for SME

The shift toward integrated accounting represents both a challenge and an opportunity for SMEs. While the path is complex, early adopters are already seeing benefits, including improved access to green finance, stronger stakeholder relationships, and operational efficiencies (Rounaghi, 2019). As Schaltegger & Burritt (2010) emphasize, the key is focusing on "decision-useful" information rather than exhaustive reporting.

Looking ahead, several trends will shape SME accounting:

- Increased standardization of sustainability metrics.
- Growth of sector-specific reporting frameworks.
- Tighter integration between financial and ESG software systems.

For SMEs, the strategic imperative is clear: begin the transition now with manageable first steps, while building capabilities for more comprehensive reporting in the future. Those who succeed will be well-positioned in an increasingly sustainability-driven business landscape.

6.4 Study Cases of SME in France: How are They Considering Non-Financial Issues?

6.4.1 SME Company: BON SPOT—A Holistic Approach to Sustainable Business Practices

6.4.1.1 About the Company

BON SPOT represents an innovative fusion of sports hospitality and sustainability. Founded in 2016 by Robin Raveneau, this unique establishment combines a climbing gym with a restaurant, transitioning from a franchise to an independent operation by 2025. With 17 full-time employees, the company has systematically integrated environmental and social responsibility into its core operations. This case study examines how BON SPOT successfully balances commercial objectives with sustainability commitments, creating a model that other small and medium enterprises might emulate.

6.4.1.2 Environmental Stewardship in Daily Operations

The company's environmental strategy focuses on two key areas: sustainable sourcing and waste management. For its restaurant operations, BON SPOT has implemented a 100% local procurement policy, ensuring all ingredients are fresh and regionally sourced. This approach significantly reduces the carbon footprint associated with food transportation while supporting local producers. In its climbing operations, the company has joined the Clean Climber France network, establishing systems for resoling climbing shoes and repurposing climbing holds. The waste management program features an innovative paid composting solution that not only processes organic waste but also includes bin washing services, creating additional hygiene benefits for the business.

6.4.1.3 Social Responsibility and Community Engagement

BON SPOT's social initiatives demonstrate a deep commitment to community development. The company actively promotes climbing as an inclusive sport, developing programs that welcome participants from diverse backgrounds and ability levels. Internally, the organization has implemented an unusual but effective HR policy: employees can dedicate 25% of their working time to projects outside their primary responsibilities. This approach has fostered innovation, staff retention, and organic development of CSR initiatives from within the workforce. The policy reflects a progressive understanding of employee engagement and its role in driving sustainable business practices.

6.4.1.4 Market Challenges and Competitive Positioning

Navigating the competitive landscape presents ongoing challenges for BON SPOT. Management recognizes that sustainability efforts are becoming a key differentiator in their sector, with some competitors already more advanced in their CSR implementations. While pursuing the ECOTABLE certification for its restaurant, the company faces financial and operational hurdles, including the requirement to increase vegetarian menu options. Current efforts focus on communicating their sustainability story to customers, though this remains a work in progress. The leadership maintains that even small, cost-effective sustainability measures can create meaningful impact while building toward more comprehensive programs.

6.4.1.5 Strategic Motivations and Implementation Barriers

Multiple factors, including regulatory requirements, economic pressures, and genuine environmental concerns, have driven the company's sustainability journey. However, this transition has not been without obstacles. High certification costs, the need to shift organizational culture, and limited human resources all present significant challenges. As Robin Raveneau notes, the key has been starting with manageable initiatives that demonstrate quick wins while laying groundwork for more ambitious projects. This phased approach has allowed BON SPOT to maintain financial stability while progressively enhancing its sustainability profile.

6.4.1.6 Transferable Lessons

BON SPOT's experience offers valuable insights for other SMEs considering sustainability integration. The company demonstrates how businesses can begin with practical, low-cost initiatives while building toward more comprehensive programs. Their success stems from aligning sustainability efforts with core operations, engaging employees in the process, and maintaining flexibility to adapt to market demands. Perhaps most importantly, BON SPOT demonstrates that sustainability in SMEs does not require perfect execution from the outset, but rather a committed and pragmatic approach that evolves with the business. This case suggests that authentic, incremental sustainability efforts can create competitive advantages while contributing to broader environmental and social goals.

6.5 Conclusion and Future Perspectives

For small and medium-sized businesses, the combination of sustainability reporting and standard financial accounting presents both a significant challenge and an opportunity for transformation. This chapter explores the evolving regulatory landscape, innovative analytical methods, and practical implementation techniques through case studies that showcase the successful integration of financial and non-financial factors. Implementing sustainability reporting systems often involves costs that outweigh the resources available to SMEs. For companies with limited specialist staff, the technical complexity of standards, with its strict disclosure requirements and double materiality assessments, creates a substantial burden. SMEs usually lack personnel with specialized knowledge of non-financial reporting, unlike large firms that often have dedicated sustainability teams.

Owner-managers must depend on external consultants or develop new skills, which adds operational difficulties.

For many SMEs, gathering reliable sustainability data across their operations remains difficult. Many smaller firms still lack the systematic methods needed to shift from anecdotal evidence to measurable metrics. SMEs hesitate because sustainability standards are changing rapidly. Due to the ongoing evolution of frameworks (from NFRD to CSRD, national laws to European standards), smaller businesses struggle to determine whether investing in reporting infrastructure will be worthwhile. The observation of some SMEs by completing our questionnaire demonstrates how proactive sustainability efforts can create new market niches, particularly when larger companies begin to prioritize the ESG performance of their supply chains. In increasingly conscious markets, early adopters gain a competitive advantage. The experience of BON SPOT highlights how transparent and honest sustainability communication builds stronger relationships with clients, staff, and community partners. Increased client loyalty, improved staff retention, and stronger community support are just a few of the tangible benefits that result from this trust. SMEs can identify and reduce risks before they lead to operational disruptions or financial liabilities by conducting a systematic review of environmental and social impacts. In risk management, early detection of sustainability-related risks provides a strategic advantage. Both case studies show how the need for sustainability can drive innovation in processes and products. Environmental restrictions often inspire innovative solutions that enhance business models and operational efficiency. SMEs with thorough sustainability reporting have better access to funding, as financial institutions increasingly consider ESG factors when deciding on loans. For established sustainable companies, green loans, sustainability-linked bonds, and impact investments offer growing opportunities. SMEs should start by identifying the sustainability issues most relevant to their specific business context, rather than attempting comprehensive reporting right away. This focused approach enables meaningful impact and efficient use of resources.

Cloud-based sustainability management software increasingly provides SME-friendly options with scalable pricing models. These solutions help streamline reporting processes, automate data collection, and include visualization features that enhance decision-making. Successful sustainable integration often takes an incremental approach, as BON SPOT has demonstrated. Starting with "quick wins" illustrates the business rationale for more ambitious projects while boosting organizational competency and motivation. An increasing number of chambers of commerce, regional business networks, and industry associations offer shared tools for sustainability reporting. These collaborative platforms facilitate peer-to-peer information sharing while reducing individual costs. Several institutional resources are available, especially for SMEs transitioning to sustainability, including financial incentives, subsidized consulting services, and technical assistance programs. Navigating this support system can significantly lower implementation barriers. Instead of viewing extra-financial reporting as a compliance requirement, successful SMEs embed sustainability considerations into their strategic planning processes. The business strategy of some specific SMEs exemplifies this integration, ensuring that reporting procedures and organizational goals are aligned. More than just a regulatory trend, the move toward integrated accounting and reporting marks a fundamental change in how business performance is perceived and measured. This shift presents SMEs with an opportunity to demonstrate how smaller, more flexible businesses can lead the way in sustainable business models. Indirect effects will increasingly influence SMEs through supply chain interactions and access to financing as the European regulatory framework evolves with the adoption of CSRD and ESRS standards. In a competitive environment where sustainability performance increasingly determines advantage, those who actively engage in these changes will find themselves in a stronger position. The case of BON SPOT illustrate how small businesses can turn regulatory demands into strategic opportunities. Their experiences demonstrate that a practical, dedicated approach tailored to the business is more crucial for successful and sustainable integration than flawless implementation from the outset. The SMEs of tomorrow that succeed will be those that see this integration as a way to develop stronger, more innovative, and meaningful business models, rather than as an administrative burden, especially as financial and non-financial aspects continue to converge. Beyond a compliance challenge, the shift to green accounting offers an opportunity to rethink how smaller businesses create, measure, and communicate value in the twenty-first century.

References

Friedman, M. (1970, September 13). The social responsibility of business is to increase its profits. *The New York Times Magazine*, 122–126.

Observatoire de la Responsabilité Sociétale des Entreprises (ORSE). (2021). *Livrable comptabilité intégrée: Un outil de transformation de l'entreprise à la portée de tous*. https://www.oree.org/wp-content/uploads/2026/01/Comptabilite_Integree.pdf

Quairel, F. (2006). Contrôle de la performance globale et responsabilité sociale de l'entreprise (RSE). In *Comptabilité, contrôle, audit et institution(s)* (pp. CD-ROM).

Quagli, A., & Paoloni, P. (2012). How is the IFRS for SMEs accepted in the European context? An analysis of the homogeneity among European countries, users and preparers in the European Commission questionnaire. *Advances in Accounting, 28*(1), 147–156. https://doi.org/10.1016/j.adiac.2012.03.002

Rounaghi, M. M. (2019). Economic analysis of using green accounting and environmental accounting to identify environmental costs and sustainability indicators. *International Journal of Ethics and Systems, 35*(4), 504–512. https://doi.org/10.1108/IJOES-03-2019-0056

Richard, J., Bensadon, D., & Rambaud, A. (2018). La comptabilité écologique: Une vraie révolution comptable? *In Comptabilité financière (11e éd.): Normes IFRS et françaises* (pp. 288–316). Dunod.

Schaltegger, S., & Burritt, R. L. (2010). Sustainability accounting for companies: Catchphrase or decision support for business leaders? *Journal of World Business, 45*(4), 375–384. https://doi.org/10.1016/j.jwb.2009.08.002

Conclusion

This book presents an exploratory analysis in which we sought to identify the foundations of a risk-profitability-sustainability balance model for SMEs (Small, and Medium-sized Enterprises) and VSEs. The objective is to develop an assessment tool that enables companies to integrate financial and non-financial indicators, thereby improving their overall performance measurement and supporting them in transitioning to a more sustainable economic model. We have initiated a reflection on the key determinants that are useful and important to consider and integrate into their production process, aiming to optimize the impact assessment of integrating non-financial approaches into their sustainable development process. Companies would benefit from a proposed and structured framework to improve their overall performance, secure their activities, attract responsible financing, and comply with increasing regulatory requirements. This book is therefore a key initiative to support SMEs in the transition to a more sustainable and resilient economy.

The three main fundamental determinants identified are: the regulatory framework, the methodological approach, and the transformation process of companies, both in terms of their improved business model and in the understanding of green and sustainable accounting approaches. The regulatory framework developed in this book encompasses the historical trajectory of the emergence and integration of CSR (Corporate Social Responsibility) approaches within the company, as well as the consideration

S. Kendo (ed.), *Non-Financial Reporting and ESG Performance*, Palgrave Studies in Impact Finance,
https://doi.org/10.1007/978-3-032-19092-5

of ESG directives defined by European standards. In addition, we presented how the reflection on non-financial reporting has evolved, with a slowdown in its practical implementation following the publication of the omnibus law on April 16, 2025. These two important aspects of the regulatory framework have raised questions about its significance for VSEs and SMEs. For VSEs, this subject remains of minor importance for this type of company, but for SMEs a huge interest.

In addition, by categorizing SMEs, particularly those with a revenue close to ETIs, and in particular those in the upper range of the revenue distribution, these various European directives are just as important for the development of one's activity. It is interesting for these SMEs to integrate them intelligently into their production process in order to provide visibility on their level of commitment to various investors and political decision-makers. In the French economy's context, numerous energy renovation programs are currently being established, with a significant share of subsidies representing a substantial contribution and providing valuable financial aid from the state to companies. Greater visibility into companies' willingness to commit to sustainability issues would give them greater access to this state financial aid.

As a result, we have identified two types of company profiles linked to the SME's development model through this study, which have therefore led to considering two underlying principles. The first principle is *intentionality*, where ESG criteria are considered from the company's inception. It means that companies commit to achieving the environmental and social objectives agreed upon with investment funds right from the start. The purpose of taking this principle of *intentionality* into account is to generate a social and/or environmental benefit explicitly. The second principle is *additionality*, where ESG criteria are integrated into a company's operating model. In other words, companies that benefit from investment funds with the achievement of E, S and G objectives, defined after the creation of the company. As a result, we have proposed a methodological approach tailored to the challenges and issues faced by SMEs in relation to the regulatory framework, investment decisions, and the various processes of transforming economic activity. By considering these two typologies, the methodological approach has facilitated a shift in thinking regarding the solutions needed for problems related to ESG measurement indicators.

Based on existing work, we have developed a reflection to evaluate ESG criteria in relation to financial criteria. There is a desire to address the issue of standardizing ESG and financial approaches by categorizing the targeted companies into two groups based on the orientations related to their development model. During our exploratory field study, we employed a decision tree to infer the combined ESG score for each of the two groups of companies. This decision tree consists of two parts: the usual ESG criteria and the controversial ESG criteria related to the sustainability of the company's activity. In the context of developing this exploratory study, the basis of our methodological analysis, we encountered specific difficulties that impacted the appropriate deployment of quantitative analysis and the description of new business models. First of all, scheduling appointments for interviews proved to be complex, requiring a significant effort to mobilize participants. Additionally, the expansion of the sample presented challenges in terms of representativeness and diversity of respondents. Access to venture capital databases has also been limited, making it more challenging to identify key players in the industry.

As a result, the feasibility and functionality of the questionnaire have been adjusted to ensure effective data collection. The relatively long duration of the interviews, estimated at around two hours, was a potential obstacle for the respondents, which affected their engagement and the quality of the answers provided. It therefore appears necessary to adapt the questions as well as the response options to the specificities of SMEs and VSEs to ensure a better match with their realities. Another major challenge lies in the lack of detailed information, particularly regarding environmental issues, which complicates the analysis of extrinsic financial impacts. Finally, it was necessary to anticipate and remedy the problems related to the absence of response, non-response, or hazardous responses, which would compromise the reliability of the results obtained.

Previous actions have led to the proposal of a practical diagnostic tool to assess the commitment and involvement of companies in addressing ESG issues. This diagnostic tool enables the assessment of a company's level of commitment to integrating ESG criteria. The diagnostic tool consists of several key components. It features a structured approach that includes a dedicated website and a questionnaire designed to evaluate company performance. The assessment is based on both financial and non-financial criteria, which encompass environmental, social, and governance (ESG) dimensions. This tool helps companies conduct an inventory of their situation, obtain a detailed assessment, and guide them towards implementing good practices in terms of sustainability and risk management. We also proposed a statistical approach inspired by the construction method of the Mazziato and Pareto composite index (MPI) to evaluate the ESG scores of SMEs. To have access to the diagnosis tool, a QR code is provided with this book for better comprehension.

Additionally, we examined various new business models and accounting approaches, including sustainability standards. Our results from this collaborative reflection include several significant achievements. A common extra-financial reference framework in line with the needs of SMEs, allowing companies and investors in the same sector to compare their financial and extra-financial performance more objectively. A beginning of a solution for the adaptation and construction of a composite index integrating financial and non-financial factors in order to provide a more complete assessment of the sustainable performance of SMEs.

This study opens the way to many fields of sustainable reflection. Companies continue to face increasing pressure to integrate ESG criteria into their strategy. SMEs, in particular, must learn how to identify, prioritize, and manage these risks in an often resource-constrained environment. In line with a more deepen collaborative think-thank, it could be possible to envision an analysis to understand which ESG risks are perceived as controllable and which appear to be challenging to manage, or even unavoidable.

Companies must also consider the three major transitions that are profoundly transforming their business models. *The ecological and environmental transition* necessitates consideration of climate risks, the implementation of energy sobriety policies, and a clear commitment to achieving carbon neutrality. At the same time, *the digital transition* raises crucial issues related to artificial intelligence, process automation, data governance, and the ethics of these technological transformations. It exposes companies to new risks (cyberattacks, data leaks, disruptions) that threaten their viability and require a transformation of their governance, management, and strategy. Ultimately, *the social transition* necessitates new forms of management and governance that are more inclusive, adaptable, and responsive to the evolving expectations of stakeholders.

Particular attention can be paid to the early stages of transition trajectories, making it possible to identify the most relevant entry points according to the size of the company, its sector of activity, its degree of maturity in terms of ESG, cybersecurity and organizational and managerial transformations, as well as its specific constraints (whether territorial, organizational, human, financial, regulatory, sectoral or technological). Identifying *when* and *where* these transitions begin or will begin is an interesting problem. To achieve this, a gradual approach is essential, taking into account the capacity to absorb these new paradigms within companies and their level of exposure to risks. This gradual process would not only preserve their economic and financial viability in the short and medium term but also lay the foundations for a more sustainable, resilient, and meaningful model.

GPSR Compliance
The European Union's (EU) General Product Safety Regulation (GPSR) is a set of rules that requires consumer products to be safe and our obligations to ensure this.

If you have any concerns about our products, you can contact us on

ProductSafety@springernature.com

In case Publisher is established outside the EU, the EU authorized representative is:

Springer Nature Customer Service Center GmbH
Europaplatz 3
69115 Heidelberg, Germany

www.ingramcontent.com/pod-product-compliance
Ingram Content Group UK Ltd.
Pitfield, Milton Keynes, MK11 3LW, UK
UKHW020936180926
475692UK00004B/75
9783032190918